AUTODESK® 3DS MAX® 8 PROJECTS WORKBOOK
REVEALED

AUTODESK® 3DS MAX® 8 PROJECTS WORKBOOK
REVEALED

Max Dutton and Jeanne Herring

THOMSON

COURSE TECHNOLOGY

Autodesk® 3ds Max® 8 Projects Workbook Revealed

Max Dutton and Jeanne Herring

Senior Acquisitions Editors:
Marjorie Hunt, James Gish

Product Manager:
Jane Hosie-Bounar

Associate Product Manager:
Shana Rosenthal

Editorial Assistant:
Janine Tangney

Production Editor:
Kelly Robinson

Developmental Editor:
Jane Hosie-Bounar

Marketing Managers:
Joy Stark, Guy Baskaran

Marketing Coordinator:
Melissa Marcoux

Compositor:
Integra—Pondicherry, India

Cover Designer:
Steve Deschene

QA Manuscript Reviewer:
John Freitas

Copyeditor/Proofreader:
Green Pen Quality Assurance

About This Revealed Series Projects Workbook

This workbook is a companion to the *Autodesk 3ds Max 8 Revealed* text. It includes a series of creative projects for additional practice of the concepts learned in the main textbook. These projects provide real-world scenarios that give students a taste of what's in store for them in the workforce, and also give students the opportunity to create and expand a portfolio of their work. Each chapter has the following features and activities:

- **Chapter Summary:** The Chapter Summary reviews the main concepts learned in the text itself.

- **Skills Reference:** The Skills Reference table lists all of the major tasks taught in a textbook chapter, and provides one or more procedures for completing each task.

- **Skills Review:** The Skills Review lets a student practice the skills learned in each lesson in a chapter, in the order they are taught.

- **Project Builders:** The Project Builders require students to apply the skills they've learned in each chapter. Project Builders often include Data Files—robust application files a student uses to start a project. Project Builders increase in difficulty from Project Builder 1 to Project Builder 3.

- **Design Project:** The Design Project lets students apply what they've learned about design to a real-world problem.

- **Portfolio Project:** The Portfolio Project combines most of the skills learned in a chapter into a single project that a student can include in his or her portfolio upon completion. The Portfolio Project gives the student leeway to use unique, creative ideas to develop or improve upon a real-world project.

- **Capstone Project:** The Capstone Project presents a scenario and a list of completion requirements. It allows students to use their individual talents and vision to combine all of the skills they've learned in the main textbook in a complex project that showcases their knowledge and talents and can be presented as the crowning achievement in a job portfolio.

CONTENTS

vii

Intended Audience

This text is designed for the beginner or intermediate user who wants to practice using 3ds Max 8. The book provides a review of each main textbook chapter, along with exercises that encourage you to explore the nuances of this exciting program.

Data Files

To complete some of the exercises in this book, you need to obtain the necessary Data Files. You can download the Data Files for the steps at the following URL: *www.course.com/ revealed/3dsmax8wb*. Once you have downloaded the files, select where to store them, such as the hard drive, a network server, or a USB storage device. The instructions in the exercises will refer to "the drive and folder where your Data Files are stored" when referring to the Data Files for the book.

Map and Texture Files

This book also uses map and texture files from 3ds Max. Depending on your version of the software, you might not have the bitmap or JPEG file suggested in the book. If this is the case, simply choose another file. Keep in mind that if you do choose another file, your screen won't match the figures in the book exactly.

1

INTRODUCING
AUTODESK 3DS MAX

1. Explore the interface.

2. Work with viewports.

3. Work with the Main toolbar.

4. Explore the Command panel.

5. Work with the track bar.

6. Customize the 3ds Max interface.

7. Use the Help menu and the Hotkey Map.

CHAPTER SUMMARY

In this chapter, you explored the 3ds Max interface and worked with some of its features. You used the Reset command to close the current file and revert the display to the default settings, and you used the New command on the File menu to choose from three options for starting a new file:

- Keep Objects and Hierarchy creates a new file with all of the current file's objects and their relationships preserved.
- Keep Objects creates a new file using the existing objects but doesn't retain their hierarchy.
- New All creates a new, blank file but does not revert 3ds Max to its default settings.

You also moved between and resized viewports. You explored the Main toolbar and the Command panel. You also used the track bar to run an animation. You customized the 3ds Max interface, applied a preset interface, and reverted to the default 3ds Max interface. Finally, you used the Help menu and Hotkey map to investigate the different options for getting Help in 3ds Max.

FIGURE 1

3ds Max scene in viewports

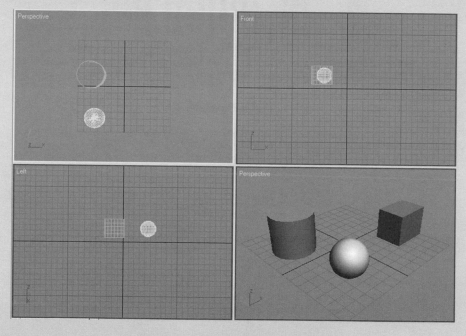

SKILLS REFERENCE

to do this:	use this method:
Activate a viewport	Click in the viewport
Add a Help topic to the Favorites panel in the User Reference	Select a topic, click the Favorites tab, then click the Add button at the bottom of the Favorites panel
Change a viewport	Activate the viewport, press [V], then click the view you want to change to **or** Activate the viewport, right-click the viewport label, point to Views, then click the viewport name you want to change to
Change the field of view in a viewport (use with caution)	⊳
Display a list of grouped tools	Click a tool with a small triangle in the bottom right, then hold down the mouse button until the list (flyout) appears
Display context-sensitive help	Press [F1] in the middle of a task
Display Help options	Click Help on the menu bar **or** Press [F1]
Display objects in a viewport as shaded	Right-click the viewport label, then click Smooth + Highlights
Display objects in a viewport as shaded with wireframe on top	Right-click the viewport label, then click Edged Faces
Display objects in a viewport as wireframe mesh	Right-click the viewport label, then click Wireframe

SKILLS REFERENCE (CONTINUED)

to do this:	use this method:
Display the Create panel	
Display the Display panel	
Display the Hierarchy panel	
Display the Main toolbar as a floating window	Right-click the far-left side of the Main toolbar, then click Float
Display the Modify panel	
Display the Motion panel	
Display the Utilities panel	
Dock the Command panel	Right-click the Command panel, point to Dock, then click Right or Left
Dock the Main toolbar	Right-click the far-left side of the Main toolbar, point to Dock, then click Top, Bottom, Left, or Right
Enter Expert mode to hide all interface elements except viewports, menu bar, and track bar	[Ctrl][X]
Expand the Command panel	Click and drag the left border of the panel where it meets the viewports
Go back one frame in an animation	
Go forward one frame in an animation	

to do this:	use this method:
Go to the first frame in an animation	⏮
Go to the last frame in an animation	⏭
Go to the next key in an animation	▶❙
Go to the previous key in an animation	❙◀
Hide or show the Command panel, floating toolbars, Main toolbar, or track bar	Click Customize on the menu bar, point to Show UI, then click Show Command panel, Show Floating Toolbars, Show Main Toolbar, or Show Track Bar
Maximize a viewport	🗗
Move an object	Click ✛ , select the object, then drag the object to its new position
Move the Main toolbar	Click and drag the Main toolbar handle to a new position
Move the viewport angle left, right, up, or down	✋
Move to a specific frame in an animation	Move the time slider to the frame number on the timeline or Enter the frame number in the Current Frame (Go To Frame) box
Open a file with which you have recently worked	Click File on the menu bar, click Open Recent, then choose from the list of recently opened files
Open a Help topic on the Contents panel	Double-click a topic name

to do this:	use this method:
Open a Help topic on the Index panel	Scroll through the topics listed, then double-click a topic **or** Type the first few letters in a topic in the Type in a keyword to find text box to jump to the topic in the Index, then double-click the topic
Open a Help topic on the Search panel	Type a keyword in the Type in the word(s) to search for text box, click List Topics, then double-click a topic
Open a new file with all objects and hierarchical relationships of the current file preserved	Click File on the menu bar, click New, click the Keep All Objects and Hierarchy option button, then click OK
Open a new file with existing objects in the current file, but not hierarchical relationships, preserved	Click File on the menu bar, click New, click the Keep Objects option button, then click OK
Open a new, blank file with current interface settings	Click File on the menu bar, click New, click the New All option button, then click OK
Open an existing file	Click File on the menu bar, click Open, navigate to the folder in which the file is located, click the file, then click Open
Open the Hotkey Map	Click Help on the menu bar, then click Hotkey Map
Open the User Reference	Click Help on the Menu bar, then click User Reference **or** Press [F1], then click User Reference
Play an animation	▶

to do this:	use this method:
Preview Custom UI schemes	Click Customize on the menu bar, then click Custom UI and Defaults Switcher
Put the Command panel in its own floating resizable window	Right-click the top of the Command panel, then click Float
Redo a change that you have undone	
Reset the interface and open a new, blank file	Click File on the menu bar, then click Reset, click Yes or No to save or not save changes you've made to the current file, then click Yes to reset
Resize a viewport	Click and drag the viewport border
Resize all four viewports at once	Click and drag the center of the screen (where all four viewports meet)
Return viewports to their default size	Right-click in the center of all the viewports, then click Reset Layout
Revert layout of interface to default when 3ds Max is started	Click Customize on the menu bar, click Load Custom UI Scheme, then click DefaultUI.ui
Revert layout of interface to layout at start of current 3ds Max session	Click Customize on the menu bar, then click Revert to Startup Layout
Rotate an object	Click , then use the rotate gizmo to rotate the object
Rotate the view of a scene around the center of a selected object	
Rotate the view of a scene around the center of a selected subobject	

Introducing Autodesk 3ds Max

SKILLS REFERENCE (CONTINUED)

to do this:	use this method:
Rotate the view of a scene around the center of the view	⌖
Save a file	Click File on the menu bar, then click Save
Save a file with a new name	Click File on the menu bar, click Save As, navigate to the folder in which you are saving the file, type a name for the file, then click Save
Save consecutive versions of the same file	Click File on the menu bar, click Save As, navigate to the folder in which you are saving the file, type a name for the file, then click the plus sign (+) to the right of the File name text box
Scale an object	Click ▢ , select the object, then drag to scale the object
Slide a toolbar left or right	Click and drag an empty space on the toolbar left or right
Stop or pause an animation	❚❚
Toggle Key mode on and off in the time controls	◄►
Travel forward, backward, up, and down, and pivot left and right in a scene	👣
Turn the grid in a viewport on or off	Click Views on the menu bar, point to Grids, then click Show Home Grid
Undo a change you have made to a file	↶
View the hotkey for a 3ds Max command	Search for the command in the User Reference, then view the hotkey next to the command in the Help topic

to do this:	use this method:
View the hotkey function of a key on the keyboard	Roll the mouse over the key on the Hotkey Map
Zoom all viewports in on a selected object or objects	
Zoom all viewports in on the objects in a scene	
Zoom in on a selected area of a scene	
Zoom in or out in a viewport	
Zoom in or out in all viewports at once	
Zoom in the active viewport on a selected object or objects	
Zoom in the active viewport on the objects in a scene	

SKILLS REVIEW

Explore the interface.

1. Click Start on the taskbar, point to All Programs, point to Autodesk, point to 3ds Max 8, then click 3ds Max 8.
2. Click File on the menu bar, then click Save.
3. Navigate to the drive and directory where your Data Files are stored, type **practice** in the File name text box, then click + (plus sign).
4. Click File on the menu bar, then click Save As.
5. In the Save File As dialog box, click + (the plus sign) to save the file as **practice02**.
6. Click the center of the screen where all four viewports meet, then drag the center until the viewports are resized, as shown in Figure 2.
7. Click the Plane button on the Create panel, then click and drag in the Front viewport to create a plane.
8. Click File on the menu bar, then click Save.
9. Click File on the menu bar, click Reset, then click Yes to reset 3ds Max.
10. Click File on the menu bar, click Open Recent, then click practice02.

FIGURE 2

Resized viewports

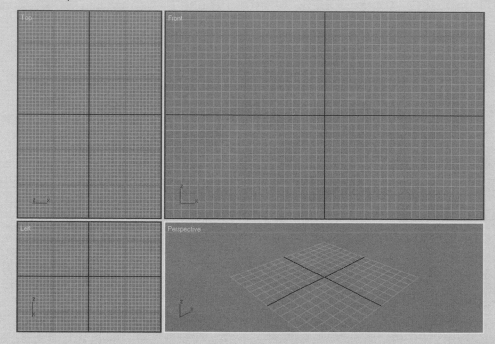

Work with viewports.

1. Right-click the Front viewport label, point to Views, then click Perspective.
2. Click the Arc Rotate button, then drag down on the top handle of the rotation trackball until the view of the plane looks like Figure 3.
3. Right-click the viewport label, then click Edged Faces.
4. Click Views on the menu bar, point to Grids, then click Show Home Grid to deselect it.
5. Click the Maximize Viewport Toggle button.
6. Click the Pan View button, then click and drag to the right and down in the viewport until the viewport looks like Figure 4.
7. Click File on the menu bar, click Save As, then click + in the Save File As dialog box to save the file as practice03.
8. Click File on the menu bar, click Reset, then click Yes to reset 3ds Max.

FIGURE 3
Arc rotated viewport

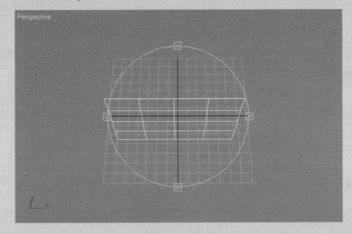

FIGURE 4
Panned viewport

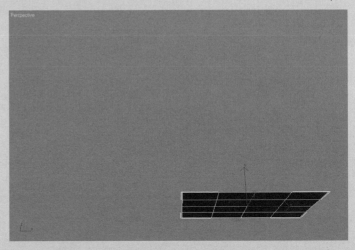

Work with the Main toolbar.

1. Move the mouse pointer over the Select and Uniform Scale tool on the Main toolbar, then click and hold down the mouse button until the Select and Uniform Scale flyout appears, as shown in Figure 5.
2. Click the Main toolbar handle on the far left side of the toolbar, then drag the toolbar so that the handle is in the center of the viewports.
3. Click and drag down the bottom border of the floating toolbar until its shape is similar to that shown in Figure 6.
4. Click and drag the right border of the floating toolbar to the right until the toolbar buttons appear in two rows.
5. Right-click a blank area of the Main toolbar, point to Dock, then click Top.

FIGURE 5
Select and Uniform Scale flyout

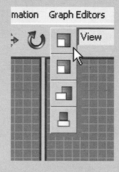

FIGURE 6
Main toolbar moved and resized

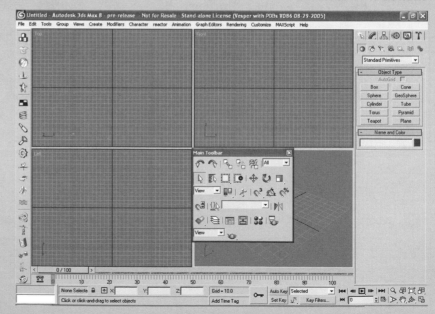

Work with the track bar.

1. Click File on the menu bar, click Open, navigate to the drive and directory where your Data Files are stored, click MAXWB01-01, then click Open.

2. Click the teapot in the Perspective viewport to select it.

3. Click the Play Animation button, watch the animation a couple of times, then click the Stop button to stop the animation.

4. Click the Go To Start button to return the animation to its beginning frame on the timeline.

5. Click and drag the time slider until the animation is at frame 40. Figure 7 shows the viewports at frame 40.

6. Click the Key Mode Toggle button, then click the Next Key button.

7. Click the Go To End button, then click the Key Mode Toggle button again to deselect it.

FIGURE 7

Animation at frame 40

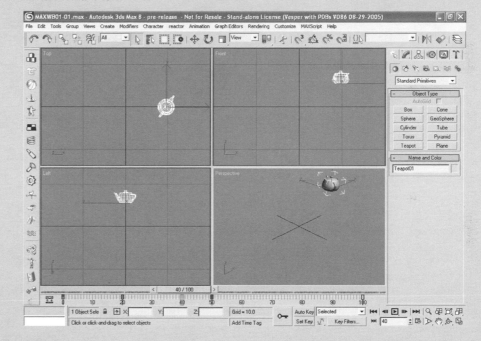

Customize the 3ds Max interface.

1. Click Customize on the menu bar, point to Show UI, then click Show Floating Toolbars. Your screen should look similar to Figure 8.

2. Click Customize on the menu bar, point to Show UI, then click Show Floating Toolbars to hide the floating toolbars.

3. Click Customize on the menu bar, then click Custom UI and Defaults Switcher.

4. Click ModularToolbarsUI under UI Schemes, click Set, then click OK.

5. Click Customize on the menu bar, click Load Custom UI Scheme, click DefaultUI.ui in the Load Custom UI Scheme dialog box, then click Open.

6. Click File on the menu bar, click Reset, click No to not save changes to the file, then click Yes to reset.

FIGURE 8

Unhidden floating toolbars

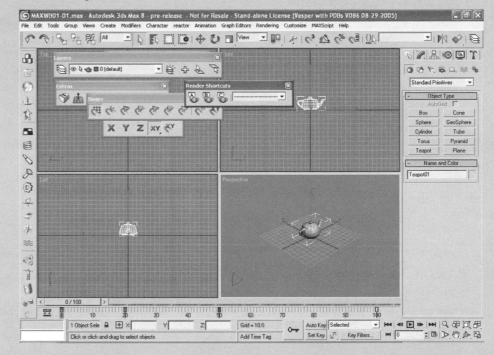

Use the Help menu and the Hotkey Map.

1. Click Help on the menu bar, click User Reference, then click the Search tab (if necessary).

2. Type **primitives** in the Type in the word(s) to search for text box, then click List Topics.

3. Double-click the Standard Primitives topic in the resulting list of topics to open it, as shown in Figure 9.

4. Click the Index tab, scroll through the list of topics until you find the "box" heading, then double-click the "standard primitive" topic underneath the "box" heading.

5. Click the 3ds Max Reference Close button.

6. Click Help on the menu bar, then click Hotkey Map.

7. Point to the letter T on the Hotkey Map, as shown in Figure 10.

8. Point to the letter M on the Hotkey Map.

9. Click the Hotkey Map Close button.

10. Click File, click Exit, then click No to close the file and to close 3ds Max.

FIGURE 9
Standard Primitives Help topic

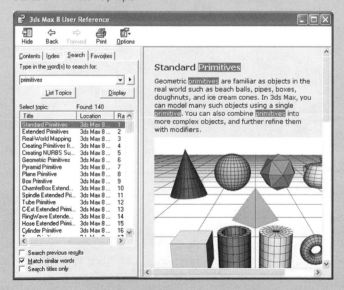

FIGURE 10
Hotkey Map

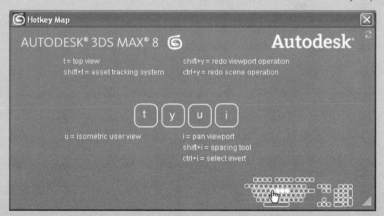

2 BUILDING AND
MODIFYING OBJECTS

1. Create standard primitives.

2. Select objects.

3. Move, rotate, and scale objects.

4. Modify a polygon object.

5. Work with segments.

6. Apply modifiers.

7. Clone objects.

8. Link and group objects.

9. Work with pivot points.

10. Use snapping tools.

11. Align objects.

CHAPTER SUMMARY

In this chapter, you created and worked with standard primitives. You selected objects in different ways using different selection tools: you selected individual objects, selected objects by name, and created a selection set to simplify the process of selecting a group of related objects. You also moved, rotated, and scaled the objects you created using the different transform gizmos available in 3ds Max. You modified objects by changing their parameters, and you learned the important role that segments play in 3ds Max. You applied modifiers to objects and worked with the modifier stack. You also cloned, linked, and grouped objects, and you created arrays of objects. You adjusted and worked with pivot points, used snapping tools, and aligned objects in a scene.

FIGURE 1
Modifiers applied to standard primitives

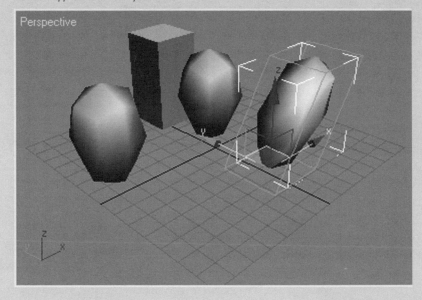

SKILLS REFERENCE

to do this:	use this method:
Align an object with another	Select a current object, click ✎ , click the target object, select the desired options in the Align Selection dialog box, then click Apply
Align objects by their centers	Select a current object, click ✎ , then click a target object
Apply a modifer to an object	Select the object, click the Modifier List list arrow on the Modify panel, then select a modifier from the list
Apply a modifier to several objects at once	Select multiple objects, click a modifier on the Modifier List, and then adjust the parameters of the modifier until the objects appear as desired
Apply an object's modifier and its parameters to another object	Select the object to which the modifier is applied, then drag and drop the modifier from the modifier stack to the second object in the viewports
Attach an object to a group	Select the object, click Group on the menu bar, click Attach, then click the group to which you want to attach the object
Break a link between objects	Select the objects, then click ⬚
Change the creation method for a standard primitive	Click the appropriate option button in the Creation Method rollout on the Create panel
Change the modifier parameters for one object in a group of objects with the same modifier applied	Select the object, click ⌣ under the modifier stack, then adjust the parameters of the modifier as needed

to do this:	use this method:
Change the number of segments on an object	Adjust the appropriate segments value in the Parameters rollout
Change the number of sides on an object	Adjust the Sides value in the Parameters rollout
Change the parameters for an object	Create an object, then change the appropriate parameter in the Parameters rollout on the Create panel **or** Select the object, then change the appropriate parameter in the Parameters rollout on the Modify panel
Change the parameters of a modifier	Select the modifier in the modifier stack, then adjust the parameters in the Parameters rollout on the Modify panel
Change the rotation or scale of links between objects	Click ⊞, click the Pivot button, select a parent object, click the Affect Hierarchy Only button, click ↻ or ▢ , then adjust the Rotate or Scale gizmo
Change the selection region shape to a circle	○
Change the selection region shape to a rectangle	▢
Change the selection region to a Fence selection region	◹

to do this:	use this method:
Change the selection region to an irregularly shaped (Lasso) selection region	
Change the selection region to select by painting objects	
Clone an object and align the clone with another object	Select the object, click Tools on the menu bar, click Clone and Align, click the Pick button, click the object(s) with which the clones should be aligned, adjust the options in the Clone and Align dialog box, then click Apply
Clone an object as a copy	Select the object, click Edit on the menu bar, click Clone, click the Copy option button, then click OK **or** Click , , or ; select the object; press and hold [Shift] while moving, rotating, or scaling the object; click the Copy option button; then click OK
Clone an object as a reference	Select the object, click Edit on the menu bar, click Clone, click the Reference option button, then click OK **or** Click , , or ; select the object; press and hold [Shift] while moving, rotating, or scaling the object; click the Reference option button; then click OK
Clone an object as an instance	Select the object, click Edit on the menu bar, click Clone, click the Instance option button, then click OK **or** Click , , or ; select the object; press and hold [Shift] while moving, rotating, or scaling the object; click the Instance option button; then click OK

to do this:	use this method:
Close an open group	Select the group, click Group on the menu bar, then click Close
Create a box	Click the Box button on the Create panel, click and drag in the viewport to create the length and width, let go of the mouse button and move the mouse pointer up or down to create the height, then click to complete
Create a cone	Click the Cone button, click and drag in the viewport to set the radius of the foundation, release the mouse button and drag up or down to create the height, click, drag up or down to set the radius of the upper surface, then click to complete
Create a cylinder	Click the Cylinder button on the Create panel, click and drag in the viewport to create the foundation, release the mouse button and drag up or down to create the height, then click to complete
Create a geosphere	Click the GeoSphere button on the Create panel, click and drag in the viewport to set the radius, then release the mouse button
Create a modifier set	Click the Configure Modifier Sets button, click Configure Modifier Sets, adjust the number in the Total Buttons box to the number of modifiers in the set, drag and drop modifiers between the lists, enter a name for the set into the Sets text box, click Save, then click OK
Create a nested group	Create a group, select the group plus an additional object or objects, click Group on the menu bar, then click Group
Create a plane	Click the Plane button on the Create panel, click and drag in the viewport, then release the mouse button to complete
Create a pyramid	Click the Pyramid button on the Create panel, click and drag in the viewport to create the foundation, release the mouse button and drag up or down to create the height, then click to complete

to do this:	use this method:
Create a selection set	Select the objects for the set, click in the Named Selection Sets box on the Main toolbar, type a name for the set, then press [Enter]
Create a sphere	Click the Sphere button on the Create panel, click and drag in the viewport to set the radius, then release the mouse button to complete
Create a teapot	Click the Teapot button, click and drag in the Top viewport to create the teapot, then release the mouse button to complete
Create a torus	Click the Torus button, click and drag in the viewport to set the outer radius, release the mouse button and drag up or down to set the inner radius, then click to complete
Create a tube	Click the Tube button, click and drag in the viewport to set the outer radius, release the mouse button and drag up or down to set the inner radius, click, drag up or down to set the height, then click to complete
Create an array in one dimension	Select an object; click Tools on the menu bar; click Array; adjust the values in the Array dialog box to create the number, type, and transformation of clones needed; then click OK
Create an array in three dimensions	Select an object; click Tools on the menu bar; click Array; adjust the values in the Array dialog box to create the number, type, and transformation of clones needed; click the 3D option button; adjust the Count number; adjust the X, Y, and Z coordinates of the cloned arrays; then click OK
Create an array in two dimensions	Select an object; click Tools on the menu bar; click Array; adjust the values in the Array dialog box to create the number, type, and transformation of clones needed; click the 2D option button; adjust the Count number; adjust the X, Y, and Z coordinates of the cloned arrays; then click OK

to do this:	use this method:
Delete a modifier from the modifier stack	Select the modifier, then click ☝ **or** Right-click a modifier, then click Delete on the right-click menu
Deselect all objects in a scene by name	Click 📑 , click the None button, then click Select
Detach an object from a group	Open the group, select the object you want to detach, click Group on the menu bar, then click Detach
Edit the contents of a selection set	⊞
Enter absolute values in the Transform Type-In boxes on the status bar (Absolute mode)	⊡
Enter offset values in the Transform Type-In boxes on the status bar (Offset mode)	⊡
Explode a group containing a nested group	Select the group, click Group on the menu bar, then click Explode
Group objects	Select the objects, click Group on the menu bar, click Group, then click OK

SKILLS REFERENCE (CONTINUED)

to do this:	use this method:
Keep a modifier active on the Modify panel no matter which object is selected (pin the stack)	Select the modifier, then click ⚑
Link objects	Click ⬚, click the object that will be the child, hold the mouse button down and drag to the object that will be the parent, then release the mouse button
Modify an object's display color	Create an object, click the color box in the Name and Color rollout on the Create panel, click a color in the Object Color dialog box, then click OK **or** Select the object, click the color box on the Modify panel, click a color in the Object Color dialog box, then click OK
Move a modifier within the modifier stack	Click and drag the modifier, then release the mouse button when the modifier is over its new location
Move a pivot point to the center of an object	Click ⬚, click the Pivot button, select the object, click the Affect Pivot Only button, then click the Center to Object button
Move an object along one of its axes	Click ✛, click the object, click and drag the corresponding axis handle in the transform gizmo
Move an object within the plane between two of its axes	Click ✛, click the object, then click and drag the square between the axes you would like to move the object between

SKILLS REFERENCE (CONTINUED)

to do this:	use this method:
Move an object's center to the location of its pivot point	Click ⬚, click the Pivot button, select the object, click the Affect Object Only button, then click the Center to Pivot button
Move or rotate a pivot point without affecting its object	Click ⬚, click the Pivot button, select the object, click the Affect Pivot Only button, then move or rotate the pivot point
Move or rotate an object without affecting its pivot point	Click ⬚, click the Pivot button, select the object, click the Affect Object Only button, then move or rotate the object
Open a group	Select the group, click Group on the menu bar, then click Open
Rename an object	Create an object, select the text in the text box in the Name and Color rollout on the Create panel, type a new name for the object, then press [Enter] **or** Select the object, select the text in the text box at the top of the Modify panel, type a new name for the object, then press [Enter]
Reorient a pivot point in relation to the home grid	Click ⬚, click the Pivot button, select the object, click the Affect Pivot Only button, then click the Align to World button
Reorient a pivot point to an object's local coordinate system	Click ⬚, click the Pivot button, select the object, click the Affect Pivot Only button, then click the Align to Object button
Reorient an object in relation to the home grid	Click ⬚, click the Pivot button, select the object, click the Affect Object Only button, then click the Align to World button

to do this:	use this method:
Reorient an object to its pivot point's axes	Click ⌘, click the Pivot button, select the object, click the Affect Object Only button, then click the Align to Pivot button
Reset a pivot point to its original location	Click ⌘, click the Pivot button, select the object, then click the Reset Pivot button
Rotate an object around one of its axes	Click ↻, click the object, then click and drag the corresponding axis handle on the transform gizmo
Rotate an object freely	Click ↻, click the object, then click and drag between the axis handles in the Rotate gizmo
Rotate an object on a plane parallel to the current viewport	Click ↻, click the object, then click and drag the outermost circle (Screen handle) in the Rotate gizmo
Scale an object along one axis while maintaining the object's visual volume	Click ▣, then click and drag the corresponding axis handle on the Scale gizmo
Scale an object along one of its axes	Click ▢. or ▢, then click and drag the corresponding axis handle on the Scale gizmo
Scale an object along two axes while maintaining the object's visual volume	Click ▣, then click and drag the corresponding plane handle between the two axes on the Scale gizmo
Scale an object along two of its axes	Click ▢. or ▢, then click and drag the corresponding plane handle between the two axes on the Scale gizmo

SKILLS REFERENCE (CONTINUED)

to do this:	use this method:
Scale an object uniformly along all axes	Click ⬜. or ⬛, then click and drag the center of the Scale gizmo
Select a selection set	Click the Named Selection Sets list arrow on the Main toolbar, then click the name of the set **or** Click ▦, click the Selection Sets list arrow, click the name of the selection set, then click Select
Select all objects in a scene by name	Click ▦, click the All button, then click Select
Select an object by name	Click ▦, click the object's name in the list, then click Select
Select an object manually	Click ▷, then click the object
Select by name all objects not currently selected	Click ▦, click the Invert button, then click Select
Select multiple objects manually	Click ▷, press and hold [Ctrl], then click each object to be selected
Select objects that are near each other in a scene	Click and drag until a selection region encloses or touches all the objects to select
Select objects that are within or cross a selection region's boundaries	⊡
Select only objects that are entirely within a selection region	⊡

Building and Modifying Objects

to do this:	use this method:
Show all modifiers applied to an object, no matter which modifier is selected	�
Turn a modifier on that has been turned off	💡
Turn off a modifier without deleting it	💡
Turn on 3D Snap	snap^3
Turn on Angle Snap	⟁
Turn on Percent Snap	$\text{snap}^\%$
Turn on Spinner Snap	snap
Ungroup objects	Select the group, click Group on the menu bar, then click Ungroup
Use Transform Type-In boxes to move, rotate, or scale an object	Click and then right-click ✛ , ↻ , ▢ , ▱ , or ▤ ; change the Absolute and/or Offset numbers in the Transform Type-In dialog box; then press [Enter] **or** Click ✛ , ↻ , ▢ , ▱ , or ▤ ; change the Absolute and/or Offset numbers in the Transform Type-In boxes on the status bar; then press [Enter]

Create standard primitives.

1. Start 3ds Max 8, click the Create tab, click the Box button, click in the upper left corner of the Top viewport, drag down and to the right, release the mouse button, drag up to create the height of the box, then click to complete.

2. Click the Cone button on the Create panel, click in the Top viewport to the right of the box's center, drag to create the radius of the base of the cone, release the mouse button, drag up to create the cone's height, click, drag down to create the radius of the top of the cone, then click to complete.

   TIP Pan or zoom out as necessary when you need more space for objects you are creating.

3. Click the Sphere button, click in the Top viewport to the right of the cone's center, drag to create a sphere, then release the mouse button.

4. Click the Base to Pivot check box at the bottom of the Create panel to align the bottom of the sphere with the bases of the box and cone.

5. Click the Cylinder button, click and drag to the right of the sphere in the Top viewport to create the cylinder's radius, release the mouse button and drag up to create the height, then click to complete. Your screen should look similar to Figure 2.

FIGURE 2

Box, cone, sphere, and cylinder

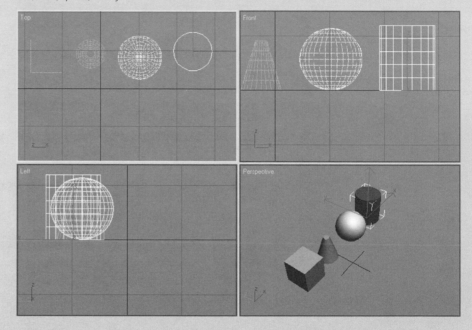

6. Click the Tube button, click and drag to the right of the cylinder in the Top viewport to create the tube's outer radius, release the mouse button and drag up to create the inner radius, click, drag up to create the height of the tube, then click to complete.

7. Click the Torus button, click and drag to the right of the tube in the Top viewport to create the outer radius, release the mouse button and drag up to create the inner radius, then click to complete.

8. Click the Pyramid button, click and drag to the right of the torus in the Top viewport to create the base, release the mouse button and drag up to create the height, then click to complete.

9. Click the Teapot button, then click and drag to the right of the pyramid in the Top viewport to create the teapot.

10. Adjust the Perspective viewport so that all objects are visible in it, as shown in Figure 3, then maximize the viewport.

11. Save the file as **Standard Primitives**.

FIGURE 3
Standard primitives

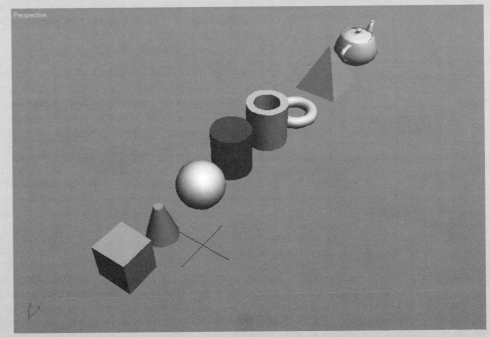

Select objects.

1. Click the Select Object tool on the Main toolbar, press and hold [Ctrl], click the box in the Perspective viewport, click each of the rest of the objects to select them, then release [Ctrl].

2. Press and hold [Alt]; click the torus object, click the pyramid, and click the tube to deselect them; then release [Alt].

3. Click the Select by Name tool, click the None button in the Select Objects dialog box to deselect all of the objects in the list, then click Select.

4. Click the Selection Region flyout, hold down the mouse button, click the Circular Selection Region tool, then click and drag to create a selection region around the box, cone, sphere, and cylinder, as shown in Figure 4.

5. Click in the Named Selection Sets text box on the Main toolbar, type **Four primitives**, then press [Enter].

6. Click away from all of the objects in the viewport to deselect them, click the Named Selection Sets list arrow, then click Four primitives.

7. Save the file.

FIGURE 4

Circular selection region

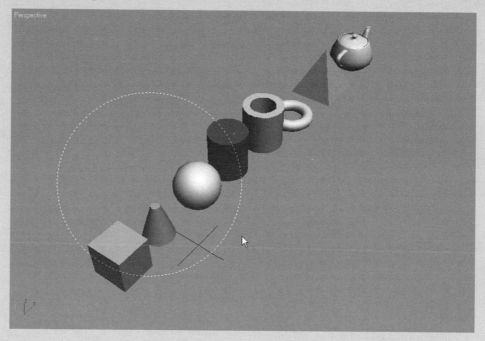

Move, rotate, and scale objects.

1. Right-click the Perspective viewport label, point to Views, then click Top.

2. Adjust the top view so that all objects are visible.

3. Click the Select and Move tool, select the box, then click and drag the green arrow down until the center of the box lines up with the viewport's original center horizontal gridline.

4. Select the cone, then click and drag the green arrow down until the horizontal center of the cone lines up with the horizontal center of the box.

5. Select each of the remaining objects, then click and drag the green arrow down until the center of each object is aligned with the other objects' centers.

6. Click the Select and Rotate tool, select the teapot, click and drag up on the blue axis handle in the Rotate gizmo until the teapot has rotated approximately 90 degrees (as shown in Figure 5), then release the mouse button.

7. Switch to the Front viewport, click the Select and Uniform Scale tool, select the cone, and then click and drag the center of the Scale gizmo up or down until the cone is the same height as the box in the viewport.

8. Select the sphere, click and drag the center of the Scale gizmo up or down until it is the same height as the box and the cone, click the Select and Move tool, then click and drag the red arrow on the Move gizmo left or right until the sphere is close to but not touching the cone.

9. Scale and move the cylinder and the tube so that they are the same height as the objects to their left and are close to but not touching the objects on their left.

FIGURE 5

Rotating the teapot

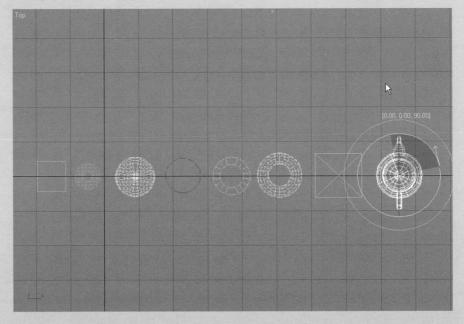

10. Click the Select and Move tool (if necessary), select the torus, drag up on the green arrow until its bottom is aligned with the bases of the other objects, then drag the red arrow left until the torus is close to but not touching the cylinder.

11. Click the Select and Uniform Scale tool, select the pyramid, scale it up or down to be the same height as the previously scaled objects, select the teapot, then scale it up or down to be the same height as the pyramid.

12. Click the Select and Move tool, right-click the Select and Move tool, then change the number in the Offset:Screen group X box in the Move Transform Type-In box to **–50**. If necessary, change the number again until the teapot is close to, but not overlapping, the pyramid.

13. Close the Move Transform Type-In box, click the pyramid to select it, press and hold [Ctrl], click the teapot to select it, release [Ctrl], then click and drag the red arrow in the Move gizmo as necessary so that the pyramid and teapot are close to but not touching the torus, as shown in Figure 6.

14. Click File on the menu bar, click Save As, then click the plus sign next to the Save button to save the file as **Standard Primitives01**.

FIGURE 6

Scaled and moved objects

Modify a polygon object.

1. Switch to the Perspective viewport, select the tube, then click the Modify tab.
2. Select the text Tube01 in the text box at the top of the Modify panel, type **Tunnel**, then press [Enter].
3. Click the color box at the top of the Modify panel, click a red color swatch in the Object Color dialog box, then click OK.
4. Select the box, then change the number in the Height box in the Parameters rollout on the Modify panel so that the box's height is doubled.

5. Select the cone, then change the number in the Radius 2 box in the Parameters rollout so that its size is doubled.
6. Select the teapot, then click the Handle and Spout check boxes in the Teapot Parts group in the Parameters rollout to deselect them.
7. Select the torus, click the Slice On check box in the Parameters rollout, change the Slice From number to **150** and the Slice To number to **190**. The line of objects should resemble that shown in Figure 7.
8. Click File on the menu bar, click Save As, then click the plus sign next to the Save button to save the file as **Standard Primitives02**.

Work with segments.

1. Minimize the Perspective viewport (if necessary), select the box in the Front viewport, then change the number in the Height Segs box in the Parameters rollout to **10**.
2. Select the cylinder, change the Cap Segments number in the Parameters rollout to **3**, then change the Sides number to **15**.
3. Select the pyramid, then change the Height Segs number in the Parameters rollout to **15**. The objects should look like those in Figure 8.
4. Save the file.

FIGURE 7
Objects with parameters modified

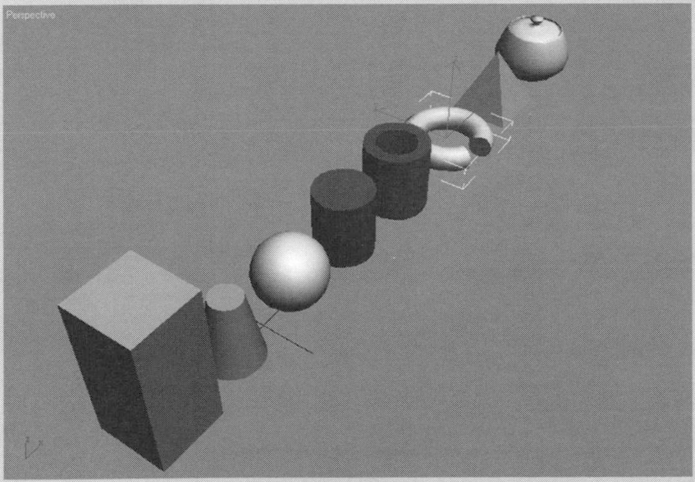

FIGURE 8
Objects with segments and sides adjusted

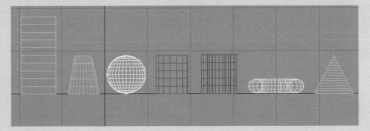

Apply modifiers.

1. Select the box in the Front viewport, click the Modifier List list arrow, then click Taper.
2. In the Taper group in the Parameters rollout for the modifier, change the Amount to **1** and the Curve to **1**.
3. Select the cone and the sphere at the same time, click the Modifier List list arrow, then click Bend.
4. In the Bend group in the Parameters rollout for the modifier, change the Angle to **–30**. The objects should look like those in Figure 9.
5. Select the cylinder and the tube at the same time, click the Modifier List arrow, then click Twist.
6. In the Twist group in the Parameters rollout for the modifier, change the Angle to **75**.
7. Select the torus, pyramid, and teapot at the same time; click the Modifier List list arrow; then click Melt.
8. In the Melt group in the Parameters rollout for the modifier, change the Amount to **35**.
9. Adjust the Perspective viewport so that it is similar to Figure 10.
10. Click File on the menu bar, click Save As, then click the plus sign next to the Save button to save the file as **Standard Primitives03**.

FIGURE 9
Bend modifier applied to cone and sphere

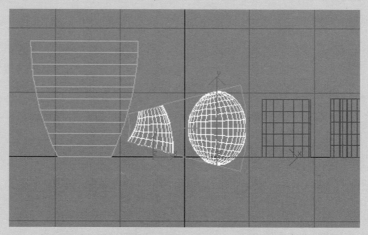

FIGURE 10
Objects with modifiers applied and adjusted

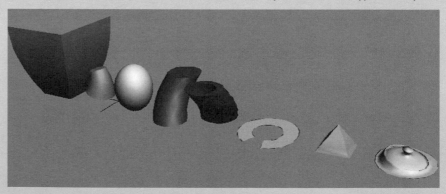

Clone objects.

1. In the Top viewport, select all of the objects in the scene.
2. Click Edit on the menu bar, click Clone, click the Copy option button in the Clone Options dialog box, select the text in the Name text box, type **Clone1**, then click OK.
3. Click the Select the Move tool, then click and drag down the green arrow to move Clone1 below the original set of objects.
4. Select the original set of objects again, press [Shift], click and drag up on the green arrow to move the cloned set of objects above the original, click the Instance option button, change the Number of Copies to **2**, then click OK.
5. Select the row of objects second from the top, click the Modifier List list arrow, then click Ripple.
6. In the Parameters rollout for the Ripple modifier, change the Amplitude 1 number to **100**, the Amplitude 2 number to **–20**, and the Wave Length to **1000**. The original set of objects and its two instances should all be affected, as shown in Figure 11.

FIGURE 11
Ripple modifier applied to instanced objects

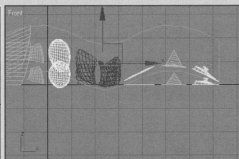

7. Select the bottom row of objects in the Top viewport, click the Select and Move tool (if necessary), press and hold [Shift], click and drag the red arrow to the right to clone a new set of objects to the right, click the Reference option button in the Clone Options dialog box, then click OK.

8. Activate, maximize, and adjust the Perspective viewport so that you can see the newly cloned reference objects, select the new set of objects, click the Modifier List list arrow, then click TurboSmooth.

9. With the reference objects still selected, click Tools on the menu bar, then click Array.

10. In the Array Objects dialog box, click the Reset All Parameters button, click the Preview button, change the number in the Count box next to the 1D option button to **1**, click the 2D option button, change the 2D Count number to **2**, then change the 2D Incremental Row Offsets Z number to **100**.

11. Click the 3D option button, change the 3D count to **3**, change the 3D Incremental Row Offsets Y number to **200**, then click OK. The array of objects should resemble that shown in Figure 12.

12. Click File on the menu bar, click Save As, then click the plus sign next to the Save button to save the scene as **Standard Primitives04**.

13. Click File on the menu bar, click Reset, then click Yes to reset 3ds Max.

FIGURE 12
Object array

Link and group objects.

1. Create a teapot and a box in the top third of the Top viewport, click the Select and Move tool, select both objects, press and hold [Shift], drag down on the green arrow in the Move gizmo to clone the objects, click the Copy option button (if necessary), change the Number of Copies to **2**, then click OK. Adjust the view (if necessary) so that you can see all six objects in the viewport.

2. Click the Select and Link tool on the Main toolbar, click the teapot in the bottom row, hold the mouse button down and drag to an edge of the box to its right, then release the mouse button.

3. Click the box in the bottom row, hold the mouse button down and drag to the box in the row above it, then release the mouse button.

4. Click the box in the middle row, hold the mouse button down and drag to the box in the row above it, then release the mouse button.

5. Switch to the Perspective viewport, adjust the view as necessary so that you can see all six objects, click the Select and Move tool, select the box in the back of the viewport, then click and drag the blue arrow up so that the linked objects move away from the other objects, as shown in Figure 13.

FIGURE 13
Moved and linked objects

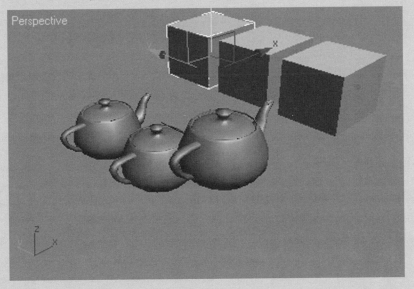

6. Select the teapot in the objects you just moved, click the Select and Rotate tool, then click the red x-axis handle on the Rotate gizmo and drag down to rotate the teapot approximately 90 degrees.

7. Click the Select and Move tool, select the box to the right of the rotated teapot, then click the blue arrow and drag down until the bottom of the box is in line with the bottoms of the unrotated teapots in the Front viewport, as shown in Figure 14.

8. In the Top viewport, click and drag to select the teapot and box in the top row, click Group on the menu bar, click Group, type **Row1** in the Group name box, then click OK.

9. Select the teapot and box in the middle row, select the Row1 group at the same time, click Group on the menu bar, click Group, type **Objects** in the Group name text box, then click OK.

10. Select the box in the bottom row, click Group on the menu bar, click Attach, then click the Objects group.

11. Click the Select and Move tool, click and drag the red arrow to move the group (and the ungrouped teapot as a child object) to the right.

12. With the Objects group selected, click Group on the menu bar, then click Explode.

13. Click File on the menu bar, then save the file as **Standard Primitives05**.

FIGURE 14
Box and child object repositioned

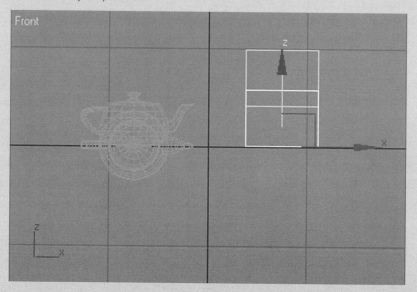

Work with pivot points.

1. Select the teapot furthest to the left in the Perspective viewport.

2. Click the Hierarchy tab, click the Affect Pivot Only button, click the Select and Move tool if necessary, then click the red arrow on the Move gizmo and drag down to drag the teapot's pivot point to the teapot's left.

3. Click the Affect Pivot Only button to deselect it, click the Select and Rotate tool, then click the blue z-axis handle in the Rotate gizmo and drag down until the teapot has rotated approximately 90 degrees, as shown in Figure 15.

4. Click the Reset Pivot button on the Hierarchy panel to return the pivot point to its original location in the teapot.

5. Click the Affect Object Only button on the Hierarchy panel, click the Select and Move tool, then click and drag the plane handle between the y- and x-axes in the Move gizmo so that the teapot is back in the location it was in before being rotated, as shown in Figure 16.

6. Click the Reset Pivot button, click the Affect Object Only button to deselect it, click File on the menu bar, click Save As, then click the plus sign to save the file as **Standard Primitives06**.

FIGURE 15
Teapot rotates around moved pivot point

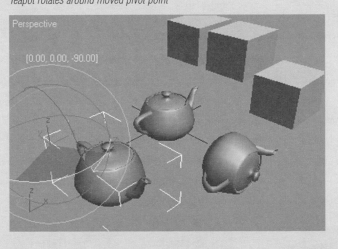

FIGURE 16
Teapot moved away from pivot point

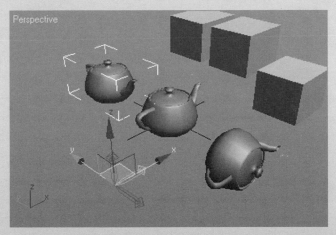

Use snapping tools.

1. Click the Angle Snap Toggle tool, click the Select and Rotate tool, select the teapot closest to you in the Perspective viewport, then click and drag the blue z-axis handle down until the teapot has rotated exactly 45 degrees.

2. Switch to the Top viewport, select the teapot in the middle row, click the Percent Snap Toggle button, click the Select and Uniform Scale tool, then click and drag up on the y-axis handle on the Scale gizmo until the scale along the y-axis increases by 50 units in the Transform Type-In Y box on the status bar.

3. Click the Snaps Toggle button, click the Select and Move tool, then click and drag the red x-axis handle on the Move gizmo 50 units to the right, as shown in Figure 17.

4. Click the Snaps Toggle button to deselect it.

FIGURE 17

Teapot moved 50 units

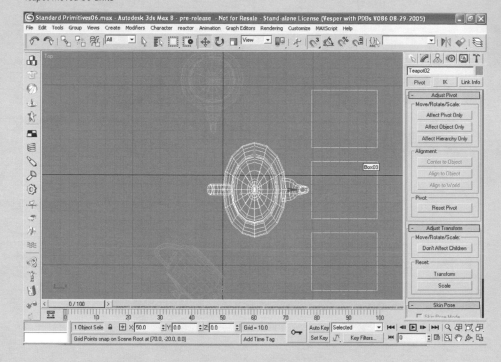

Align objects.

1. In the Top viewport, select the teapot in the middle row, click the Align tool on the Main toolbar, then click the teapot in the top row.
2. In the Align Selection dialog box, click the Y Position check box to deselect it, then click the X Position check box to select it.
3. Click the Maximum option button in the Current Object group to align the middle teapot's maximum with the top teapot's center.
4. Click the X Axis check box in the Align Orientation (Local) group to align the center teapot with the orientation of the top teapot, then click OK.
5. Click the teapot in the bottom row, click and hold down the mouse on the Align tool, click the Quick Align tool on the flyout, then click the teapot in the top row.
6. Select the teapot in the middle row, click Tools on the menu bar, click Clone and Align, then click the Pick button at the top of the Clone and Align dialog box.
7. Click the box in the middle row, click the box in the bottom row, click Apply, then click Cancel to close the Clone and Align dialog box. The Top viewport should now look like Figure 18.

8. Click File on the menu bar, click Save As, then click the plus sign next to the Save button to save the file as **Standard Primitives07**.
9. Click File on the menu bar, click Reset, then click Yes to reset 3ds Max.

FIGURE 18
Cloned and aligned teapots

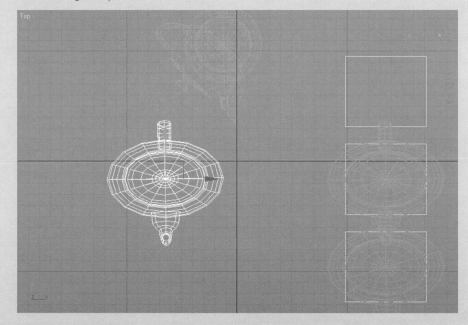

You work for a film company effects department. One of the films currently in production depicts a young man working in an Italian restaurant, daydreaming about an army of ziti (pasta tubes) coming to life and marching forward across a table. You are assigned the task of creating the army of ziti that can be animated and included in the film for the daydreaming sequence. To create the army, you plan to make multiple instances of a single primitive, and then add the appearance of a swaying type of movement to give the army a lifelike appearance.

1. In the Top viewport, create a tube with parameters of $30 \times 25 \times 175$, name the tube **Ziti**, then recolor it with a color similar to the color of pasta.
2. Click the Select and Move tool, press and hold [Shift], move the ziti to the right in the Perspective viewport, then click the Instance option button and change the Number of Copies to at least **20** in the Clone Options dialog box.
3. Select the entire row of ziti, then clone the row to create at least five instanced rows of ziti to serve as the army formation.
4. Select one of the Ziti, apply the Bend modifier to it, then adjust the Angle parameter for the modifier up and down to see how the ziti might sway when animated.

5. Set the final Angle for the Bend modifier to −**33**, as shown in Figure 19.
6. Save the file as **Ziti**, then reset 3ds Max.

FIGURE 19
Completed Project Builder 1

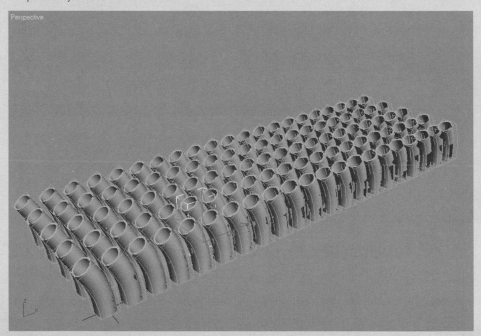

You work for an advertising agency and are part of a team that produces animation used in television commercials. Your latest commercial is part of an overall campaign for a major tea company. The campaign shows how the teapots in which the tea is brewed really enjoy the tea. In the TV commercial, the client wants the teapot to look as though it is elatedly blowing out steam. You are prepared to show the client representatives a number of ways you can make the teapot look alive and excited, in case they aren't satisfied with the first example they see, and you plan to produce a visual they can review showing the appearance of the teapot at different stages of the animation.

1. Create a teapot sitting on a plane.
2. Apply the Stretch modifier to the teapot, then adjust the Stretch and Amplify parameters for the modifier up and down to create the look of a teapot breathing in and out over time (this shows what is possible; the teapot is not actually animated).
3. Remove the Stretch modifier from the teapot, then apply the Bend modifier to the teapot.
4. Adjust the Angle parameter for the Bend modifier up and down to create the look of the teapot bending back and forth.
5. Apply the Push modifier to the teapot, then increase and decrease the Push Value for

the modifier to create the look of the teapot breathing in and out.
6. Return to the Bend modifier and adjust both the Angle and Direction parameters for the modifier to see the kinds of looks you can create.
7. Set the parameters for the Bend and Push modifiers so that the teapot looks like it is inhaling while leaning backwards, about to blow off steam.
8. Make three copies of the teapot, increase the size of the plane and move it so that all four teapots are sitting on the plane, then adjust

the perspective view so that all four teapots are seen from the front left.
9. Turn on Spinner Snap, select the teapot on the far left, then decrease the Push Value parameter for the teapot's Push modifier by 9 units.
10. Select the teapot second from the left, then decrease the Push Value for its Push modifier by 6 units.
11. Decrease the Push Value for the teapot second from the right by 3 units. The teapots should resemble Figure 20.
12. Turn off Spinner Snap, save the file as **Teatime**, then reset 3ds Max.

FIGURE 20
Completed Project Builder 2

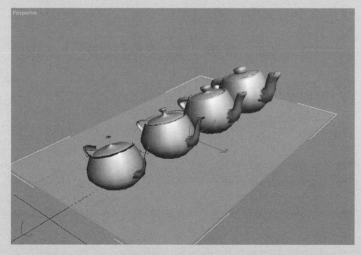

PROJECT BUILDER 3

In your position in the design department of an advertising agency, you are responsible for coming up with graphic images used in print ads for clients. A campaign for a doughnut company that is a client of the agency is going to depict doughnuts so hot that they melt as they come off of a conveyer belt. The art director has asked you to create a still image of a dozen doughnuts in a partly melted state

1. Create a torus shaped like a plump doughnut resting on a plane.
2. Recolor the torus so that it looks like a plain doughnut and recolor the plane a light color (if necessary).
3. Change the number of segments in the torus to **50**, change the number of sides in the torus to **25**, then apply the Melt modifier to the torus.
4. Turn on 3D Snap; create three copies of the torus to form a line of four doughnuts evenly spaced apart; then create two instances of each torus in the line, so that there are twelve doughnuts total arranged in four rows of three.
5. Turn off 3D Snap, then resize and move the plane as necessary so that the group of doughnuts is centered on the plane, as shown in Figure 21.

FIGURE 21

Arrangement of doughnuts on plane

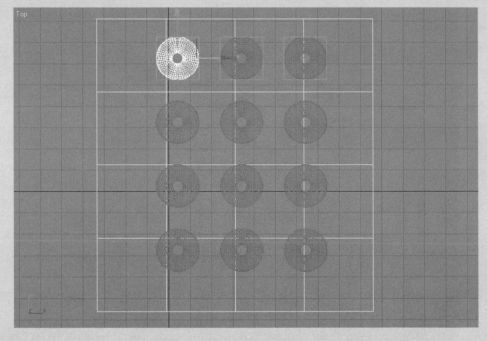

Building and Modifying Objects

6. Modify the doughnuts so that the first row of three does not look melted at all; the second row looks partly melted; the third row looks more melted; and the fourth row is almost, but not quite, totally melted. Try entering a Custom number in the Solidity group on the Melt modifier's Parameters rollout to get the look you want. The scene should look similar to Figure 22.

7. Group each row of three doughnuts together—naming the groups **Row1**, **Row2**, **Row3**, and **Row4**—then create a group of all twelve doughnuts called Dozen.

8. Link the plane as a child object to the Dozen group.

9. Save the file as **Glazed**, then reset 3ds Max.

FIGURE 22
Completed Project Builder 3

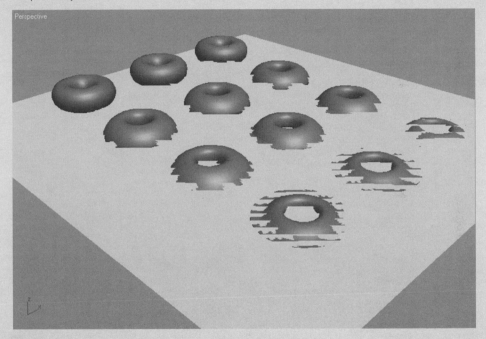

DESIGN PROJECT

When you learn how to draw, the first thing you learn how to do is to draw a smiley face and a stick figure—the basics. Building a scene with standard primitives in 3ds max is similar to working with stick figures when drawing. The detail isn't there, but you can still use them to design an environment and indicate approximations of the items you want to be in a scene. In this exercise, you'll create an outdoor scene using primitives to represent items in the scene.

1. Create a plane in the Top viewport to serve as the ground in the scene.

2. Create a tall tube on the plane, create several spheres, then arrange them into the shape of a tree.

3. Create a long and slender plane that resembles a road next to the tree, then apply a modifer to the plane that makes the road curved. Increase the segments in the road as necessary to get the curve you want.

4. Create a cone in the scene that is some distance from the tree and road, apply a smoothing modifier to it, and apply other modifiers or parameter changes as desired to create the look of a peaked hill.

5. Clone the hill and edit the clones so that a range of hill sizes appears in the scene.

6. Create a boulder in the scene by applying the Noise modifier to a sphere, selecting the modifier's Fractal check box, and adjusting the Strength values.

7. Group the objects that make up the tree together, then make multiple copies of the group and insert the trees around the scene.

8. Make copies of the boulder and insert the boulders around the scene. Figure 23 shows an example of what your completed scene might look like.

9. Save the scene as **Street**, then reset 3ds Max.

FIGURE 23
Example of completed Design Project

PORTFOLIO PROJECT

You work in the Marketing department of a planetarium outside of a big city. One of the ways the planetarium markets to schools is by offering classes to young students about different astronomy topics. A scientist at the planetarium is planning a class about the solar system, and has asked you to create the graphics for the class. She wants you to create a solar system that can be animated, in which the sun and planets are represented by spheres. She would like the display colors of the planets to be fairly accurate, and she wants the planets to be placed in the correct order leading away from the sun. In addition, she wants the appropriate relationships between the planets and the sun so be in the file so that the different revolutions of the planets around the sun can be animated during the class.

1. Research the solar system using books or online resources. Be sure to locate information about the size of each planet, color, and distance from the sun.
2. Create a sphere for the sun and for each planet in the solar system. Name each accordingly.
3. Use a standard primitive to show Saturn's rings, then group the rings and sphere.
4. Size each planet as large, medium, or small, according what your research has turned up.

Make the sun three times the size of a large planet.
5. Change the sun and each planet's display color to be close to the real color of each.
6. Position the planets in a line leading away from the sun, in order, from the planet closest to the sun to the planet farthest from the sun. Use snapping tools to put the same number of units between each planet and the next in the line.

7. Link each planet to the sun as a child object of the sun, rotating each planet away from the line of planets after you complete each link. When all links are completed, render the scene. See Figure 24 for an example of a completed scene.
8. Save the file as **Solar System**, then reset 3ds Max.

FIGURE 24
Example of completed Portfolio Project

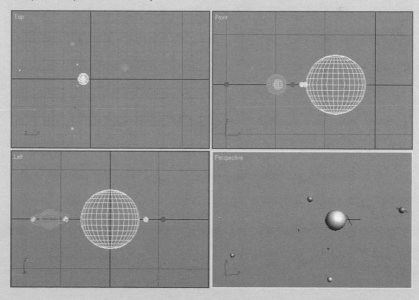

3 MODELING

1. Understand editable polygons.

2. Apply modifiers to subobjects.

3. Understand normals.

4. Chamfer, extrude, and bevel objects.

5. Use Paint Deformation and Soft Selection.

6. Create and connect vertices, edges, and polygons.

7. Model efficiently.

8. Model a character.

9. Understand splines.

10. Edit splines.

11. Model with splines.

CHAPTER SUMMARY

This chapter focused on modeling with objects as editable polygons (polys) and editable splines. You learned how to convert an object into an editable poly so that you could work with it more efficiently. You selected the subobject levels of an editable poly, and applied modifiers to those subobjects to affect just part of the object's appearance or behavior. You welded, sliced, and cut objects while modeling. You also learned about normals, and how they work in 3ds Max. You learned how to model with a reference, so that a change to the original object results in a change to the reference. You also created, edited, and modeled with splines, essential tools for many of the tasks you perform as you work in a scene. Most importantly, you learned how to use your knowledge thus far to create a character.

FIGURE 1
Modeled object from Chapter 3

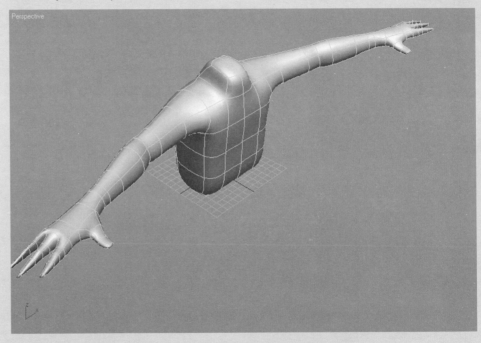

SKILLS REFERENCE

to do this:	use this method:
Apply modifiers to different subobjects in the same editable poly	Select and apply a modifier to one set of subobjects, apply the Mesh Select modifier to the parent object, select the new subobject level in the Mesh Select Parameters rollout, then select and apply a modifier to the second set of subobjects
Apply modifiers to subobjects	Select the subobjects, click the Modifier List list arrow, click the modifier name
Apply the Lathe modifier to a spline	Create a line spline, apply the Lathe modifier to the spline, adjust the modifier's center (if necessary), then flip the object's normals (if necessary)
Bevel a polygon	Select the subobject, click the Bevel button, click and hold the mouse button while dragging the polygon up or down to extrude it, release the mouse button, drag up or down to bevel the polygon, then click to set the bevel **or** Click the Settings button next to the Bevel button, change the Height amount and the Outline amount, then click OK
Bridge two borders	Select two borders, then click the Bridge button **or** Click the Bridge button, click one border, then click a second border
Bridge two polygons	Select two polygons, then click the Bridge button **or** Click the Bridge button, click one polygon, then click a second polygon

SKILLS REFERENCE (CONTINUED)

to do this:	use this method:
Chamfer a vertex, edge, or border	Select the subobject, click the Chamfer button, then click and drag the selected subobject up or down
Convert a spline segment into a curved line	Right-click a selected segment between two smooth, Bezier, or Bezier Corner vertices, then click Curve
Convert a spline segment into a straight segment	Right-click a selected segment between any two vertices, then click Line
Convert a spline to an editable spline	Right-click the spline, point to Convert To, then click Convert to Editable Spline or Right-click the name of the object in the modifier stack display on the Modify panel, then click Editable Spline in the Convert To list on the right-click menu
Convert a spline vertex into a corner, smooth, Bezier, or Bezier Corner vertex	Right-click a selected vertex, then click Corner, Smooth, Bezier, or Bezier Corner
Convert all of a spline's vertices to corner or Bezier vertices	In the Spline subobject level, right-click the spline, then click Line or Curve
Convert an object into an editable poly	Right-click the object, point to Convert To, then click Convert To Editable Poly or Right-click the name of the object in the modifier stack display on the Modify panel, then click Editable Poly in the Convert To list on the right-click menu
Create a circle	Click the Circle button, click at the location of the circle's center, hold the mouse button down and drag to set the radius, then release the mouse button

to do this:	use this method:
Create a closed line spline (shape)	Click the Line button, click once, move the mouse, click again, continue until all vertices are created, click the starting vertex, then click Yes
Create a donut	Click the Donut button, click at the location of the donut's center, hold the mouse button down and drag to set the outer radius, release the mouse button and drag to set the inner radius, then click again
Create a helix	Click the Helix button, click and drag to set the radius of the bottom of the helix, release the mouse button and drag up to set its height, click, then drag to create the radius of the top of the helix, then click again
Create a loft object starting with a path	Select the path object, click the Loft button, click the Get Shape button, then click the object you want to be the shape
Create a loft object starting with a shape	Select the shape object, click the Loft button, click the Get Path button, then click the object you want to be the path
Create a new edge in Edge or Border subobject level	Click the Create button, click a vertex, then click another (unconnected) vertex in the same polygon **or** Select two edges in the same polygon, then click the Connect button
Create a new edge in Vertex subobject level	Select a vertex, select another (unconnected) vertex in the same polygon, then click the Connect button
Create a new polygon between isolated or border vertices	In Polygon or Element subobject level, click the Create button, click one of the isolated or border vertices, click the other vertices you need to create the edges of the polygon, then return to the first vertex and click it

to do this:	use this method:
Create a rectangle	Click the Rectangle button, click at the location of one corner of the rectangle, hold the mouse button down and drag to the location of the rectangle's opposite corner, then release the mouse button
Create a star	Click the Star button, click the location of the star's center, hold the mouse button down and drag to set the radius of the outer points, release the mouse button and drag to set the radius of the inner points, then click again
Create a text spline	Click the Text button, click a location for the center of the text, then edit the text in the Parameters rollout
Create an arc	Click the Arc button, click and hold the mouse button down, drag to the endpoint vertex's location, release the mouse button, then drag up or down to adjust the arc's radius
Create an ellipse	Click the Ellipse button, click once, hold the mouse button down and drag to set the length and width, then release the mouse button
Create an NGon	Click the NGon button, click the location of the NGon's center, hold the mouse button down and drag to create the radius, then release the mouse button
Create an open line spline (path)	Click the Line button, click once, move the mouse, click again, continue until the spline is complete, then right-click
Cut an object	Click the Cut button, click at a point on the object's surface, click again to create an edge between clicks, move the pointer and click again as desired, then right-click

to do this:	use this method:
Enter Vertex, Edge, Border, Polygon, or Element subobject level	∴ , ◁ , 𝒪 , ■ , or ▰ **or** Click the plus sign next to Editable Poly in the modifier stack display, then click Vertex, Edge, Border, Polygon, or Element
Enter Vertex, Segment, or Spline subobject level	∴ , ⌃ , or ⌄ **or** Click the plus sign next to Editable Spline in the modifier stack display, then click Vertex, Segment or Spline
Extrude a spline	Select the spline, apply the Extrude modifier to it, then adjust the Amount number in the modifier's Parameters rollout
Extrude a vertex, edge, border, or polygon	Select the subobject, click the Extrude button, then click the subobject and drag up or down **or** Click the Settings button next to the Extrude button, change the Extrusion Height amount, then click OK
Flip normals in an object	Apply the Normal modifier to an object
Insert a Bezier vertex into a spline	Click the Insert button, click a location on the spline, click and drag to place a Bezier vertex there or move the mouse and click and drag to place a vertex elsewhere, then right-click
Insert a corner vertex into a spline	Click the Insert button, click a location on the spline, click to place a vertex there or move the mouse and click to place a vertex elsewhere, then right-click

to do this:	use this method:
Insert a vertex in Edge or Border subobject level	Click the Insert Vertex button, then click a location on the edge or border
Insert a vertex in open space	In Vertex subobject level, click the Create button, then click a location in space
Insert a vertex in Polygon or Element subobject level	Click the Insert Vertex button, then click a location on a polygon
Modify spline parameters	During or just after spline creation, use the Parameters rollout on the Create panel **or** Select an existing spline, then use the Parameters rollout on the Modify panel
Paint soft-selection on an object	Click the Paint button in the Paint Soft Selection group, then click and drag on the object
Pull vertices	Click the Push/Pull button in the Paint Deformation rollout, then click and drag over the vertices to be pulled
Push vertices	Click the Push/Pull button in the Paint Deformation rollout, press and hold down [Alt], then click and drag over the vertices to be pushed
Relax vertices	Click the Relax button in the Paint Deformation rollout, then click and drag over the vertices to be smoothed

to do this:	use this method:
Revert pulled or pushed vertices	Click the Revert button in the Paint Deformation rollout, then click and drag over the vertices to be reverted
Slice an object	Click the Slice Plane button, adjust the slice plane gizmo's position, then click the Slice button **or** Click the QuickSlice button, click on one side of the object, and then click on the other side of the object
Soft-select a vertex or vertices	Click the Use Soft Selection check box in Soft Selection rollout, then select the vertex or vertices
Weld one vertex to another vertex's location	Click the Target Weld button, click the vertex you want to move, then click the vertex to which you want to weld the first vertex
Weld vertices at the midpoint between them	Select two vertices, then click the Weld button

Modeling

SKILLS REVIEW

Create editable polygons.

1. In the Top viewport, create a cylinder with a radius of 10 and a height of 300, change the number of Height segments and Sides both to **20**, then change the number of Cap Segments to **1** (if necessary).
2. Right-click the cylinder, point to Convert To on the Transform quadrant of the Quad menu, then click Convert To Editable Poly.
3. Adjust the Front viewport so you can see the entire cylinder, click the Vertex button in the Selection rollout on the Modify panel, then click and drag to select all of the vertices in the cylinder except those on the top and bottom of the cylinder.
4. Click the Select and Uniform Scale tool, then click the green dot on the Scale gizmo and drag down until the rows of vertices in the cylinder appear as shown in Figure 2.
5. Click the Select and Move tool, then click the green arrow on the Move gizmo and drag the vertices up until the top row of selected vertices is very close to the top of the cylinder.
6. Save the scene as **Cane**.

FIGURE 2

Scaled vertices

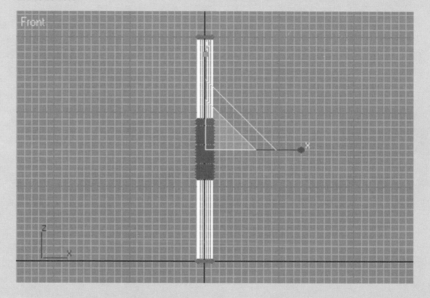

Apply modifiers to subobjects.

1. Select all of the vertices in the top half of the cylinder, including those on the top.
2. Click the Modifier List list arrow on the Modify panel, click Bend, then change the Angle value in the Parameters rollout to **180**.
3. Click the plus sign next to Bend in the modifier stack, then click Center.

4. Click the Select and Move tool (if necessary), then click the green dot on the Move gizmo and drag down until the center is even with the bottom selected row of vertices.
5. Click the Modifier List list arrow on the Modify panel, then click Edit Poly.
6. Click the Vertex button in the Selection rollout on the Modify panel, then in the

Front viewport, select the row of vertices around the top circumference of the cane.
7. Click the green dot on the Move gizmo, then drag down until the tip of the cane looks like that shown in Figure 3.
8. Save the file, then reset 3ds Max.

FIGURE 3

Completed cane

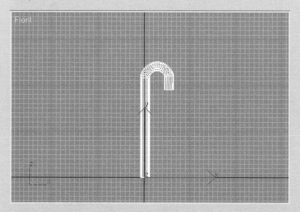
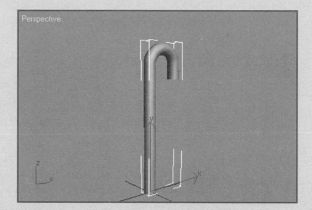

View and flip normals.

1. In the Top viewport, create a plane, teapot, and a sphere next to each other.
2. Click in the Perspective viewport, click the Arc Rotate button, drag within the view rotation trackball until the view shows the teapot from above, click the Zoom button, then zoom in on the teapot until you see the spout showing through the gap between the lid and the top of the teapot.

3. Zoom out from the teapot, click the Arc Rotate button, then drag within the view rotation trackball again until the view shows the objects from underneath and the plane is invisible.
4. Drag within the view rotation trackball until you can see the objects side by side, select the sphere, right-click it, point to Convert To, then click Convert to Editable Poly.
5. Click the Vertex button in the Selection roll-out on the Modify panel, select the vertices

in the top half of the sphere, then press [Delete] to delete the top half of the sphere.
6. Click the Modifier List list arrow on the Modify panel, then click Normal to flip the normals in the sphere.
7. Click the Arc Rotate button, then drag within the view rotation trackball to view from different angles the appearance of the sphere with its normals flipped, as shown in Figure 4.
8. Save the file as **Normals**, then reset 3ds Max.

FIGURE 4
Half sphere with normals flipped

Chamfer, extrude, and bevel objects.

1. In the center of the Top viewport, create a square plane with the dimensions 115 × 115, 4 length segments, and 4 width segments.

2. Right-click the plane, point to Convert To on the Transform menu, click Convert to Editable Poly, then click the Polygon button on the Modify panel.

3. Press [Ctrl], then click each of the four polygons around the center point of the plane to select them.

4. Click the Select and Uniform Scale tool, in the Top viewport click the plane handle between the y- and x-axes in the Scale gizmo, then drag up to increase the size of the four selected polygons uniformly until they appear as shown in Figure 5.

5. Click in the Perspective viewport, press [F4] to show Edged Faces in the viewport, then zoom out a bit in the viewport.

6. Select the four polygons again, click the Settings button next to the Extrude button in the Edit Polygons rollout on the Modify panel.

7. In the Extrde Polygons dialog box, change the Height number to 40, click Apply, change the Height number to 5, then click Apply.

8. Change the Height to 40, click Apply, change the Height to 5, click Apply, change the

Height to 40, click Apply, change the Height to 5, click Apply, change the Height to 40, click Apply, change the Height to 5, click Apply, then click Cancel to exit the Extrude Polygons dialog box. The box should now look like a four-story building.

9. With the polygons still selected, click the Settings button next to the Bevel button in the Edit Polygons rollout on the Modify panel.

10. In the Bevel Polygons dialog box, change the Height to 0 and the Outline amount to –10, click Apply, change the Height to –5 and the Outline amount to 0, then click Apply to create the look of a roof for the building.

11. In the Front viewport, press and hold [Ctrl] while clicking and dragging to select the top three rows of large polygons in the building, as shown in Figure 6.

FIGURE 5
Polygon with scale increased

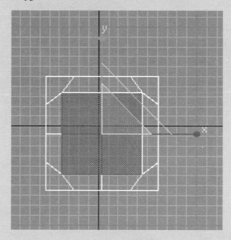

FIGURE 6
Selected polygons

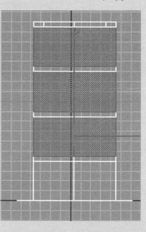

12. In the Bevel Polygons dialog box, click the By Polygon option button, change the Height to –2, change the Outline Amount to –5, click Apply, then click Cancel to close the dialog box.

13. Save the file as **Building**.

14. Click the Vertex button in the Selection rollout on the Modify panel, select the vertex at the center of the roof, then click the Settings button next to the Chamfer button in the Edit Vertices rollout on the Modify panel.

15. In the Chamfer Vertices dialog box, change the Chamfer Amount to 20, then click OK.

16. Click the Polygon button in the Selection rollout on the Modify panel, select the polygon just created by chamfering the vertices, then click the Settings button next to the Bevel button in the Edit Polygons rollout on the Modify panel.

17. In the Bevel Polygons dialog box, click the Group option button, change the Height to 10 and the Outline Amount to 0, click Apply, change the Height to 0 and the Outline Amount to –5, click Apply, change the Height to 10 and the Outline Amount to –3, click Apply, change the Height to 0, click Apply, change the Height to 40 and the Outline Amount to –2, then click OK to create an antenna on the top of the building.

18. Click the Edge button in the Selection rollout on the Modify panel, select the edge between the two large polygons on the right side of the first level of the building, click the Chamfer button, then click and drag up until the chamfered edges look like a door on the bottom floor of the building.

19. Click the Polygon button in the Selection rollout, click the polygon created by the chamfered edges, click the Extrude button in the Edit Polygons rollout, then click the selected polygon and drag down to create the look of a doorway at the bottom of the building. At this point, the building should look like that in Figure 7.

20. Save the file, then reset 3ds Max.

FIGURE 7
Completed building

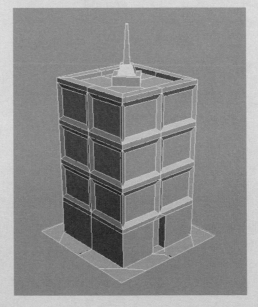

Use Paint Deformation and Soft Selection.

1. In the Top viewport, create a 200×200 plane with 25 Length segments and 25 Width segments, then convert the plane into an editable poly.
2. Click the Vertex button in the Selection rollout on the Modify panel, pan the Modify panel up until you see the Paint Deformation rollout, open the rollout (if necessary), then click the Push/Pull button to select it.
3. Maximize the Perspective viewport, then zoom out until you can see the whole plane in the viewport.
4. If necessary, make sure that the Push/Pull Value is **10**, the Brush Size is **20**, and the Brush Strength is **1**; then click and drag to pull vertices on the plane, and press [Alt] while you click and drag to push vertices. Although it won't match exactly, try to create the same type of terrain shown in Figure 8. Remember that pulling the same vertices multiple times pulls them more each time.
5. In the Paint Deformation rollout, click the Relax button to select it, then click and drag along the sharp peaks created by pulling vertices on the plane to dull them.

FIGURE 8
Plane with pushed and pulled vertices

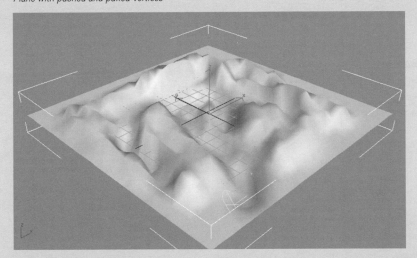

6. In the Paint Deformation rollout, change the Brush Size to **30**, click the Revert button, then click and drag the paintbrush inside one of the corners of the plane to revert its vertices to their original positions, as shown in Figure 9.

7. Change the Brush Size back to **20**, click the Revert button to deselect it, then click the Commit button.

8. Save the file as **Terrain**, then reset 3ds Max.

9. In the Top viewport, create a sphere with a radius of 50, then convert it into an editable poly.

10. Click in the Front viewport, maximize it, then click the Vertex button in the Selection rollout on the Modify panel.

11. Click the plus sign next to the Soft Selection rollout (if necessary), then click the Use Soft Selection check box to select it.

12. Select the top vertex and the horizontal row of vertices below it in the Front viewport, then increase the Falloff value in the Soft Selection rollout until the vertices in the sphere range from red at the top to blue in the middle and bottom half, indicating their degree of soft selection.

13. Click the Select and Move tool, click the green y-axis arrow on the Move gizmo, then drag up to move the selected and soft-selected vertices until the sphere's shape looks like an egg, as shown in Figure 10.

14. Save the file as **Egg**, then reset 3ds Max.

FIGURE 9
Completed terrain

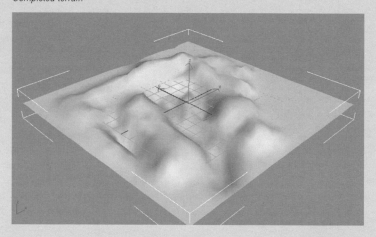

FIGURE 10
Completed egg

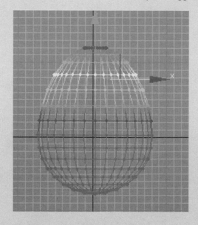

Create and connect vertices, edges, and polygons.

1. Create a box in the Top viewport that has 1 length segment, 1 width segment, and 1 height segment, then convert the box to an editable poly.

2. Click the Edge button in the Selection rollout on the Modify panel, then click the Insert Vertex button in the Edit Edges rollout.

3. In the Perspective viewport, click once in the center of the top edge of the polygon on the right, then click once in the center of the bottom edge below it to create two new vertices.

4. Click the Vertex button in the Selection rollout, select both new vertices (if necessary), then click the Connect button in the Edit Vertices rollout.

5. Click the Polygon button in the Selection rollout, click the Cut button in the Edit Geometry rollout, click once in the center of the polygon on the left of the new edge, click once in the center of the polygon to the right of the new edge, then right-click.

6. Click the Cut button to deselect it, click the Element button in the Selection rollout, select the box, click the Slice Plane button in the Edit Geometry rollout, rotate the slice plane gizmo 90 degrees around its x-axis, click the Slice button, then click the Slice Plane button to deselect it. The box should now look like Figure 11.

FIGURE 11
Cut and sliced box

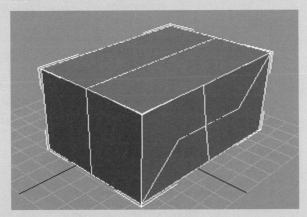

7. Click the Polygon button in the Selection rollout, click the polygon on top of the box closest to you in the viewport, click the Extrude button, then click and drag up about an inch to extrude the polygon.

8. In the Front viewport, select and delete the new polygons created by the extrusion, leaving the extruded polygon remaining above the box.

9. Click the Border button in the Selection roll-out, click the border of the extruded polygon in the Perspective viewport, press [Ctrl] and click the border of the hole on top of the box, then click the Settings button next to the Bridge button in the Edit Borders rollout.

10. In the Bridge Borders dialog box, change the Segments to **6** and Twist 1 to **2**, then click OK. The box should look like Figure 12.

11. Save the file as **BoxTwist**, then reset 3ds Max.

Model efficiently.

1. In the Top viewport, create a box with a length of 95, width of 50, and height of 15, containing 3 length segments, 4 width segments, and 1 height segment.

2. Convert it into an editable poly.

3. Click the Select and Move tool, press and hold [Shift] while moving the box to the right, click the Reference option button in the Clone Options dialog box, then click OK.

4. With the reference (Box02) selected, click the Modifier List list arrow on the Modify panel, then click TurboSmooth.

5. Save the file as **Handwrist**.

FIGURE 12
Bridged borders

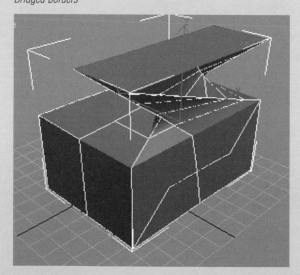

Model a character.

1. Zoom and arc rotate in the Perspective viewport until you can see the top of Box01.
2. Select the original object (Box01), click the Polygon button in the Selection rollout on the Modify panel, press and hold [Ctrl], then click to select all four polygons at the top of Box01, as shown in Figure 13.
3. Click the Settings button next to the Bevel button in the Edit Polygons rollout on the Modify panel, click the By Polygon option button in the Bevel Polygons dialog box, then click OK.
4. Click one of the selected polygons, then extrude and bevel the polygons until they resemble fingers, as shown in Figure 14.
5. Click in the Left viewport, click the Vertex button in the Selection rollout, then move the vertices in the fingers as necessary to adjust the curvature of the hand. (Remember that when you select a row of vertices in the Left viewport, you select all of the vertices behind that row).
6. In the Top viewport, adjust the vertices individually to distinguish the fingers from each other in size and the direction each points.

FIGURE 13
Selected polygons

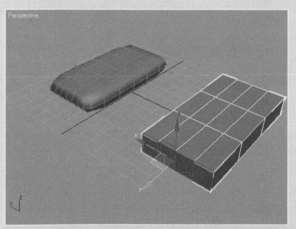

FIGURE 14
Polygons extruded and beveled to resemble fingers

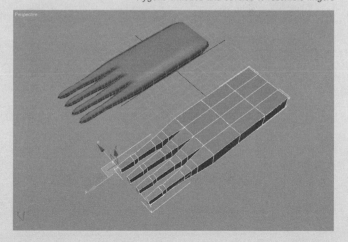

Modeling

7. Click the Polygon button in the Selection rollout, click in the Perspective viewport, then, on the side of Box01, select the polygon second from the right.

8. Rotate the polygon around its z- and y-axes so that it extends away from the rest of the box and points downward.

9. Extrude and bevel the polygon to get the right amount of segments for the thumb, as shown in Figure 15.

10. Click the Vertex button, then move, rotate, and scale the vertices for the thumb and the palm of the hand, relying on the reference copy to see the effect of your modifications and make the results as realistic as possible.

11. Click the Polygon button, select the polygons at the base of the hand (the wrist), click the Settings button next to the Extrude button, click the Group option button in the Extrude Polygons dialog box, click OK, then click and drag the polygons twice to extrude them and create the segments for a lower forearm.

12. Click the Vertex button, then move the vertices on the wrist and lower forearm in the Top viewport until they resemble Figure 16.

13. Save the file, then reset 3ds Max.

FIGURE 15
Polygon extruded and beveled to resemble thumb

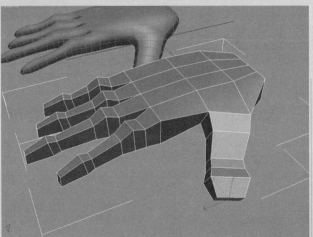

FIGURE 16
Completed hand and wrist

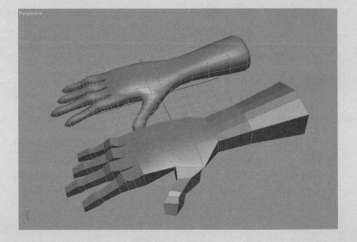

Create splines.

1. Click the Shapes button on the Create panel, then click Line in the Object Type rollout.

2. Click in the upper left quadrant of the Top viewport, move the mouse down, click, move the mouse right, click, move the mouse up, click, move the mouse to the location of your first click, click, then click Yes to close the spline, as shown in Figure 17.

Edit splines.

1. Maximize the Top viewport, click the Modify tab, click the Vertex button in the Selection rollout, click the Select and Move tool, then click the upper left vertex in the spline and move it to the left.

2. Right-click the upper left vertex, then click Smooth on the Tools 1 quadrant of the Quad menu.

3. Right-click the upper right vertex in the spline, click Bezier on the Tools 1 quadrant of the Quad menu, then click the lower Bezier handle and move it to change the shape of the curve through the vertex.

4. Right-click the bottom right vertex in the spline, click Bezier Corner on the Tools 1 quadrant of the Quad menu, then click and move both Bezier handles on the vertex until the segments connected to the vertex look like those in Figure 18.

FIGURE 17
Closed spline

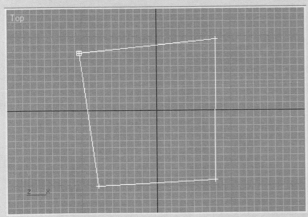

FIGURE 18
Spline with vertices converted

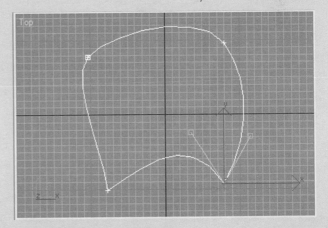

5. Click the Segment button in the Selection rollout on the Modify panel, click the segment connecting the top right and bottom right vertices on the spline, press [Ctrl], then click the segment connecting the top left and bottom left vertices on the spline.

6. Right-click one of the selected segments, then click Line on the Tools 1 quadrant of the Quad menu to change both segments to straight lines, as shown in Figure 19.

7. Save the scene as **Closedspline**, then reset 3ds Max.

Model with splines.

1. Click in the Front viewport, click the Maximize Viewport button, click the Pan button, then drag within the viewport to move the center of the grid to the lower left corner.

2. Click the Snaps Toggle tool on the main toolbar to select it, click the Shapes button on the Create panel, click the Line button, click and drag within the viewport to create the spline shown in Figure 20, right-click after creating the last vertex, then click the Snaps Toggle tool to deselect it.

3. Click the Modify tab, click the Vertex button in the Selection rollout, then change the vertices in the spline indicated in Figure 20 so that they are smooth.

FIGURE 20
Created spline

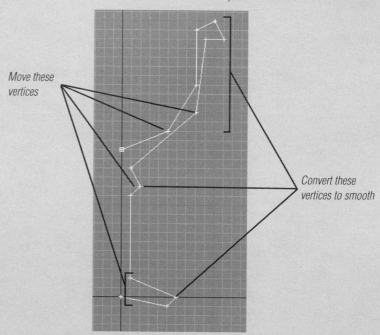

Move these vertices

Convert these vertices to smooth

FIGURE 19
Spline with edges converted

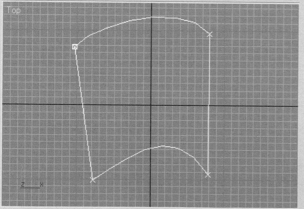

4. Move the vertices indicated in Figure 20 so that the spline looks like Figure 21.
5. Click the Modifier List list arrow on the Modify panel, then click Lathe.
6. Click the plus sign next to Lathe in the modifier stack display, click the Axis sub-object, click the red arrow handle on the Move gizmo in the Front viewport, then move the handle to the left until the axis lines up with the vertical dark line on the left side of the viewport.
7. Click the Flip Normals check box in the Parameters rollout on the Modify panel to flip the normals in the object (if necessary), then change the Segments number in the parameters rollout to 30. The object in the Perspective viewport should look like Figure 22.
8. Save the file as **Goblet.max**, then reset 3ds Max.

FIGURE 21
Edited spline

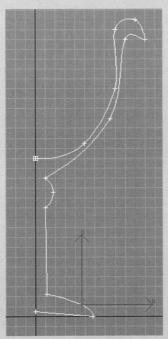

FIGURE 22
Completed goblet

You are an industrial designer for a home goods manufacturer. You are part of a team designing dinnerware, and your first task is to design a decorative bottle that can be used as a decanter for beverages. To give the bottle an interesting shape and detail, you decide to use a loft object in 3ds Max to create the design.

1. In the Top viewport, create a circle spline with a radius of 40 and a rectangle spline with a length of 75 and a width of 95.

2. Maximize the Front viewport, then create the line spline shown in Figure 23.

3. Maximize the Perspective viewport, click the Geometry button on the Create panel, click the list arrow beneath the Geometry button, click Compound Objects, then, with the line selected in the viewport, click Loft in the Object Type rollout.

4. Click the Get Shape button in the Creation Method rollout, then click the circle in the viewport to extrude it along the path.

5. In the Path Parameters rollout on the Create panel, change the Path number to **20**, click the Get Shape button in the Creation Method rollout, then click the rectangle to extrude it along the path starting at 20% of the distance along the path.

6. Click the Modify tab, click the plus sign next to Loft in the modifer stack display, click Shape, click the Angle Snap Toggle button, click the Select and Rotate tool, click the line in the loft object indicating the location of the rectangle shape, then click and drag the blue rotate handle to the left until there is no twist between the circle at the bottom of the object and the rectangle.

7. Click the Select and Move tool, click the circle at the bottom of the Loft object, press [Shift], drag up on the z-axis handle of the Move gizmo to move a duplicate of the circle along the path to a point halfway between the circle and rectangle shapes, click the Instance option button in the Copy Shape dialog box if necessary, then click OK.

8. Click the Select and Uniform Scale button, then reduce the scale of the circle so that the bottom of the object looks like Figure 24.

FIGURE 23
Spline path

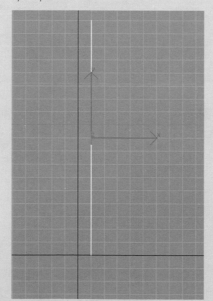

FIGURE 24
Scale of circle reduced

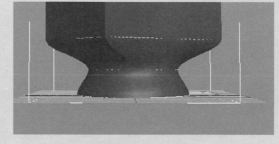

9. Make instances of the circle and rectangle shapes, then move, re-scale, and rotate them as necessary until the loft object resembles that shown in Figure 25.

10. Select the original rectangle shape (Rectangle01), click the Modify tab, then change the Corner Radius in the Parameters rollout to 4 to round the corners of the loft object.

11. Click Loft in the modifier stack display, open the Skin Parameters rollout on the Modify panel, then click the Cap End check box to deselect it and give the loft object a hollow look.

12. Apply the Shell modifier to the loft object, then, in the Parameters rollout on the Shell modifier's Modify panel, change the Inner Amount to **1** and the Outer Amount to **0** to give the loft object some thickness, as shown in Figure 26.

13. Save the file as **Decanter**, then reset 3ds Max.

FIGURE 25
Object with new shapes inserted and moved

FIGURE 26
Completed decanter

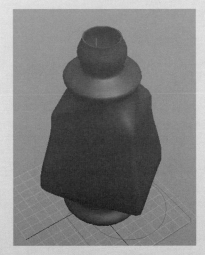

Modeling

You recently picked up a freelance job for an interior designer who has asked you to design a chess set to be included in the redesign of a client's living room. You decide to create the king piece in the chess set and then base the design of the rest of the pieces on the king.

1. Maximize the Front viewport, click the Snaps Toggle button, then, starting from the top, create a line spline, moving and converting its vertices as necessary, so that the spline looks like Figure 27.

2. Apply the Lathe modifier to the spline, move the modifier's center as necessary, then flip the normals in the modifier (if necessary) so that the result looks like a pawn piece from a chess set.

3. Maximize the Perspective viewport, convert the object into an editable poly, then adjust the view in the viewport so that you can see the top of the chess piece.

4. Switch to the Top viewport, then (if necessary) select and weld the vertices at the center of the top of the chess piece so that there is a single vertex at the top.

5. Chamfer the top vertex on the chess piece to create a small circle on top of the chess piece, then extrude the circle to create a thin cylinder on top of the piece.

6. In the Front viewport, use the Slice Plane tool to slice the cylinder horizontally at a point about 3/5 the way up the cylinder, and then again about 4/5 the way up the cylinder.

FIGURE 27
Line spline with edited vertices

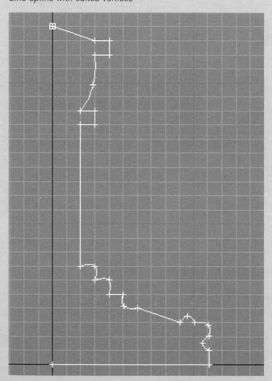

7. In the Front viewport, select the polygons shown in Figure 28 between the edges created by the slices, then, in the Edit Polygons rollout on the Modify panel, click the X button next to the Make Planar button to flatten the selected polygons with their normals facing along the x-axis.

8. Select the polygons on the opposite side of the cylinder, then click the X button next to the Make Planar button to flatten those as well.

9. Select both sets of flattened polygons in the Front viewport by clicking the vertical edge of one set, pressing [Ctrl], then clicking the edge of the other set.

10. Extrude the polygons to create a cross on top of the king's crown.

11. Slightly chamfer the edges along the top and bottom of the base of the king piece's crown, then very slightly chamfer the top and bottom edges of the king's collar.

12. Select every other edge in the circle surrounding the base of the cross on the crown, then move them down a bit to create a textured look. The completed king piece should look like Figure 29.

13. Save the scene as **Chessking**, then reset 3ds Max.

FIGURE 28
Selected polygons

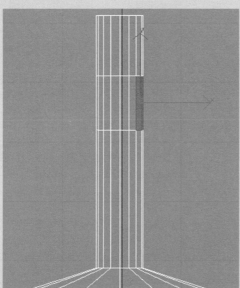

FIGURE 29
Completed king chess piece

You work for a gaming company and have been asked to create a character – part rabbit, part human - for a new game. The character should have the overall appearance of a human but with rabbit-like features such as long ears. You decide to start by creating the character's head.

1. In the Top viewport, create a sphere with a radius of 80 and 16 segments, then convert it into an editable poly.

2. In the Front viewport, select the polygons in the left half of the sphere and delete them, apply the Symmetry modifier to the sphere, then apply the TurboSmooth modifier to the sphere.

3. Move the vertices and polygons on the right side of the sphere so that the final result looks similar to a human head, as shown in Figure 30.

4. Select and extrude the polygon indicated in Figure 30 into the sphere to create eye sockets for the character.

5. Extrude, move, and rotate a polygon from the top of the head to create rabbit-like ears for the character, then move vertices in the ears to give them life-like shape.

6. Select polygons on the underside of the ears and negatively extrude them to create a concave look, as shown in Figure 31.

7. Chamfer the upper corners of the border of the eye socket, pull the polygon between the chamfer-created polygons forward to create a brow over the socket, extrude the eye socket polygon a bit more to hollow the socket further, then move vertices and polygons to build up a nose and a chin.

8. Right-click the Symmetry modifier in the modifier stack display, then click Collapse To to collapse the editable poly and modifier together so that the whole object is editable and is no longer affected by the Symmetry modifier.

FIGURE 30
Object edited to resemble head shape

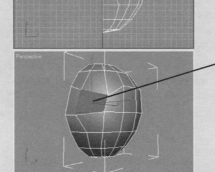

Eye socket polygon

FIGURE 31
Ears on character

9. Chamfer the edges on the character's face where the mouth should be to create a mouth shape, chamfer the outline of the mouth to create lip polygons, then extrude the lip polygons a bit, as shown in Figure 32.

10. Select the vertices on the outer corners of the mouth and the inner corners of the extruded lip polygons, then weld them to the vertices behind them.

11. To the right and left of the center edge of the top lip, use the QuickSlice button to create edges, then edit the vertices to create the mouth shape shown in Figure 33.

12. Select and scale the vertices in the mouth to decrease its width and increase its height, so that the mouth is in a neutral open position.

13. Extrude and bevel the polygons on the interior of the mouth to create a deeper cavity.

14. Fine tune the model further so that it resembles Figure 34 as closely as possible.

15. In the Front viewport, create two spheres identical in size, then move them (and scale them, if necessary) so that they fit into the eye sockets as shown in Figure 34.

16. Save the file as **Rabbitman**, then reset 3ds Max.

FIGURE 32
Extruded mouth

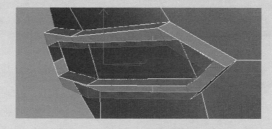

FIGURE 33
Mouth detail added

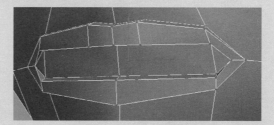

FIGURE 34
Completed head of character

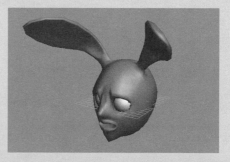

DESIGN PROJECT

You are working for a feature film company special effects department. A movie in production is going to include a shot of a glass on a table exploding. However, the plan is to simulate the glass exploding in order to minimize cost and danger to the actors in the movie. The explosion itself is going to be generated by someone else in the department, but you are charged with creating the glass to be used in the simulation. To make sure that the glass looks realistic and that you translate the proportions of the real glass accurately into 3ds Max, you decide to use a picture of the actual glass displayed in the viewport background as a reference.

1. Find a digital picture or illustrated image of a distinct piece of glassware, shown in profile, and then download the image. If you have or can create your own digital photo of the profile of an object, you can use that instead. You can use clip art from the Web that is free for both personal and commercial use (check the copyright information for any such clip art before downloading it).

2. In 3ds Max, select the Front viewport, click Views on the menu bar, click Viewport Background, click the Files button in the Background Source group in the Viewport Background dialog box, navigate to the object image in the Select Background Image dialog box, then click Open.

3. In the Aspect Ratio group in the Viewport Background dialog box, click the Match Bitmap option button, click the Lock Zoom/Pan check box to the right, then click OK to open the image in the background of the Front viewport.

4. Using the image in the Front viewport background as a reference, create a line spline that traces the profile of the object in the image. Remember to trace around half of the profile, including the interior of the glass. Using the image of a real object should enable your model to closely match its real proportions. Save the scene as **Glassware**.

5. When you have traced the profile of the object, click Views on the Menu bar, click Viewport Background, then click the Display Background check box to deselect it and remove the image from the Front viewport background.

6. Delete, move, and convert the vertices in the spline to make its shape match that of the glass as closely as possible. If necessary, redisplay the image of the glass (click the Display Background check box in the Viewport Background dialog box to select it) to fine tune the shape of the spline.

7. Apply the Lathe modifier to the spline, re-center it, and then flip its normals.

8. Redisplay the image in the Front viewport background and compare the object you created with that shown in the photo. Make any adjustments necessary to the object to increase its realism, then save the file and reset 3ds Max. An example glass and its source image are shown in Figure 35.

FIGURE 35

Example of completed glass and photo reference

Photo courtesy of Mark Battista

PORTFOLIO PROJECT

You are working for an advertising agency that is planning an animated commercial for a battery company generated in 3ds Max. They plan to feature items in the commercial that demonstrate what kinds of items the batteries "electrify!" Your assignment is to create a flashlight that will be used in the animation.

1. For the body of the flashlight, create a loft object using a circle and a straight line. Make copies of the circle within the loft object and scale and move the circles to create the form of the flashlight.

2. Delete the polygon at the end of the loft object to create an opening for the light.

3. Create and position standard primitive objects that serve as the rim of the light cavity and a cap on the base.

4. Create and position a half sphere within the light cavity that serves as the bowl containing the light, flip its normals, then create and position a small sphere representing the flashlight bulb in the bottom of the half sphere.

5. Create, position, and model two boxes along the side of the flashlight to create the flashlight switch.

6. Change the display colors in the flashlight to give it more realistic coloring. An example flashlight is shown in Figure 36.

7. When you've completed the flashlight model, save the file as **Flashlight**, then reset 3ds Max.

FIGURE 36
Example of completed flashlight

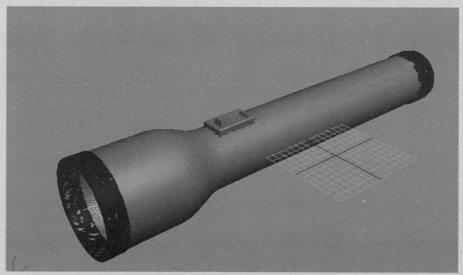

4 MATERIALS AND
MAPS

1. Understand materials.

2. Apply materials.

3. Edit materials.

4. Understand and assign maps.

5. Navigate materials and maps.

6. Map basic shader components.

7. Map other Standard material components.

CHAPTER SUMMARY

In this chapter, you applied materials to objects so that they responded to light in a realistic way, conveying realistic depth, distance, texture, color, and shadow. You edited materials using the Material Editor to get a desired effect. You learned about the most commonly used shaders in 3D animation, and worked extensively with the Blinn shader. You learned what maps are in 3ds Max and used maps to further control the appearance of a material's components. You also navigated between maps and materials as you worked on a scene by using the Material/Map Navigator.

FIGURE 1
Reflection maps assigned to object materials

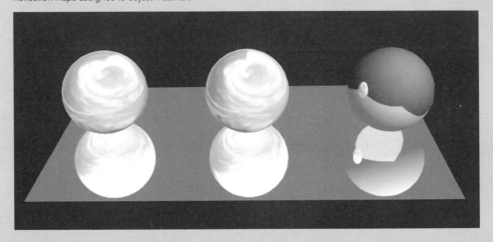

If you are using 3ds Max 6 or 3ds Max 7 to complete these exercises, you may not have some of the maps and materials referred to in the exercises. If this is the case, simply choose a different map or material that is available in your release to complete the exercise. Note that choosing a different map or material will cause your scenes to vary from those shown in the figures.

SKILLS REFERENCE

to do this:	use this method:
Add a sample multicolored background to a sample slot	▨
Adjust the index of refraction of a material	Adjust the number in the Index of Refraction box in the Advanced Transparency group of the Extended Parameters rollout
Apply a material to an object in a scene	Click the sample slot showing the material, drag it over the object in the viewport, then release the mouse button **or** Select the object to which the material is to be applied, select the sample slot containing the material, then click ⌗
Apply maps to the face of each polygon in the objects to which a material is applied	Click the Face Map check box in the Shader Basic Parameters rollout for the material
Apply material to both sides of the faces in an object	Click the 2-Sided check box in the Shader Basic Parameters rollout for the material
Apply material to the wireframe of an object	Click the Wire check box in the Shader Basic Parameters rollout for the material
Assign a bitmap from outside 3ds Max to a material	Double-click the Bitmap map in the Material/Map Browser to open the Select Bitmap Image File dialog box, browse to the location of the file you want to use as the map, select the file, and then click the Open button

to do this:	use this method:
Assign a map to a material so that it automatically refracts the light that passes through it	Click the Refraction map button in the Maps rollout, then double-click the Reflect/Refract map in the Material/Map Browser
Assign a map to a material so that the material reflects its surrounding environment	Click the Reflection map button in the Maps rollout, then double-click the Reflect/Refract map in the Material/Map Browser
Assign a map to a material to give it a bumpy look	Click the Bump map button in the Maps rollout, then double-click the map that you want to use to define the bumps
Assign a map to a material whose image you want to be reflected by the material	Click the Reflection map button in the Maps rollout, double-click the Bitmap map to open the Select Bitmap Image File dialog box, browse to the location of the file you want reflected, select the file, and then click Open
Assign a map to a material whose image you want to be refracted by the material	Click the Refraction map button in the Maps rollout, double-click the Bitmap map to open the Select Bitmap Image File dialog box, browse to the location of the file you want refracted, select the file, and then click Open
Assign a map to a Standard material component	Click the map button to the right of the component's Amount spinner box in the Maps rollout, then double-click the map in the Material/Map Browser **or** Click ☐ next to the component in the Blinn Basic Parameters rollout, then double-click the map in the Material/Map Browser

to do this:	use this method:
Assign a map to another map	In the parent map's Parameters rollout, click the map button, then double-click the submap in the Material/Map Navigator
Assign a map to a material that appears on a flat object so that it reflects like a mirror	Click the Reflection map button in the Maps rollout, double-click the Flat Mirror map in the Material/Map browser, then apply the mapped material to a flat surface
Assign an image or pattern to a material to give the object multiple filter colors	Click the Filter map button in the Extended Parameters rollout or click the map button next to Filter Color in the Maps rollout, then double-click a map in the Material/Map Browser
Change the ambient color of a material	Click the color swatch next to Ambient, select the color in the Color Selector dialog box, then click Close
Change the diffuse color of a material	Click the color swatch next to Diffuse, select the color in the Color Selector dialog box, then click Close
Change the material used in the active sample slot	Double-click a material in the Material/Map Browser **or** Click and drag a material from the Material/Map Browser to the material Type button **or** Click and drag a material from the Material/Map Browser to the active sample slot
Change the name of a material	Select the text in the material Name field, then type the new name

to do this:	use this method:
Change the shader applied to a material	Click the Shading list arrow in the Shader Basic Parameters rollout for the material, then click the name of the shader
Change the shape used in a sample slot to a box	
Change the shape used in a sample slot to a cylinder	
Change the shape used in a sample slot to a sphere	
Change the specular color of a material	Click the color swatch next to Specular, select the color in the Color Selector dialog box, then click Close
Copy a map from one component to another as a copy	Click and drag from the first component's map button to the second component's map button, click the Copy option button, then click OK
Copy a map from one component to another as an instance	Click and drag from the first component's map button to the second component's map button, click the Instance option button, then click OK
Deactivate a map while keeping it assigned to a component	Deselect the check box to the left of the component in the Maps rollout
Increase or decrease the brightness of a material's specular highlight	Increase or decrease the material's Specular Level

to do this:	use this method:
Increase or decrease the opacity of a material	Increase or decrease the material's Opacity in the Blinn Basic Parameters rollout for the material
Increase or decrease the self-illumination of a material	Increase or decrease the material's Self-Illumination in the Blinn Basic Parameters rollout for the material **or** Click the Color check box of the Self-Illumination area of the Blinn Basic Parameters rollout for the material, click the color swatch that appears to its right, select a color with a Value number appropriate for the self-illumination level you seek, then click Close
Increase or decrease the size of a material's specular highlight	Increase or decrease the material's Glossiness in the Blinn Basic Parameters rollout for the material
Lock two color components together	
Navigate from a map to a sibling map	 **or** Click the sibling map in the Material/Map Navigator
Navigate from a map to its parent material	Click the map Name field list arrow, then click the material name **or** **or** Click the material in the Material/Map Navigator
Open a sample slot in its own resizable window	Double-click the sample slot

SKILLS REFERENCE (CONTINUED)

to do this:	use this method:
Open the Material Editor	⚬⚬ **or** Press [M] **or** Click Rendering on the menu bar, then click Material Editor
Open the Material/Map Browser	Click the material Type button **or** ⚬
Open the Material/Map Navigator	⚬
Remove a map from a component	Select the map, click the map Type button, then double-click NONE in the Material/Map Browser
Render a scene	⚬.
Select a map in the Material Editor	Click the map's button in the Maps rollout **or** Click M next to the map's component in the Blinn Basic Parameters rollout **or** Click the map in the Material/Map Navigator
Select a material in the Material Editor	Click the sample slot containing the material

to do this:	use this method:
Select a sample slot to work in	Click the sample slot
Show 15 sample slots in the Material Editor	Right-click a sample slot in the Material Editor, then click 5 × 3 Sample Windows
Show 24 sample slots in the Material Editor	Right-click a sample slot in the Material Editor, then click 6 × 4 Sample Windows
Show 6 sample slots in the Material Editor	Right-click a sample slot in the Material Editor, then click 3 × 2 Sample Windows
Show a map in the viewport	
Show the polygons in the geometry of the objects to which a material is applied	Click the Faceted check box in the Shader Basic Parameters rollout for the material
Swap maps between components	Click and drag from the first component's map button to the second component's map button, click the Swap option button, then click OK
Turn off backlighting in the active sample slot	

Understand and apply materials.

1. In the Top viewport, create a plane, create a teapot in the top center of the plane, then create a line of three copies of the teapot below the original.
2. Click Rendering on the menu bar, then click Material Editor.
3. Right-click the upper left sample slot in the Material Editor, then click 6 × 4 Sample Windows.
4. Click the upper left sample slot (if necessary), select the text in the material Name field, type **Sample 1**, then press [Enter].
5. Click the Get Material button, then double-click Raytrace in the Material/Map Browser.
6. Click and hold the Sample Type button, then click the Cylinder button.
7. Double-click Standard in the Material/Map Browser, click and hold the Sample Type button, then click the Sphere button.
8. Click the slot to the right of the Sample 1 slot, select the text in the material Name field, type **Sample 2**, then press [Enter].
9. Click the slot to the right of the Sample 2 slot, select the text in the material Name field, type **Ground**, then press [Enter].
10. Click and drag the Sample 2 sample slot over the bottom teapot in the Top viewport, release the mouse button, click and drag the Sample 2 sample slot over the teapot second from the bottom, then release the mouse button.

11. Select the top two teapots, click the Sample 1 sample slot, then click the Assign Material to Selection button.
12. Select the plane, click the Ground sample slot, then click the Assign Material to Selection button. The scene should look like Figure 2.
13. Save the file as **MaterialSamples**.

FIGURE 2

Materials applied to teapots and plane

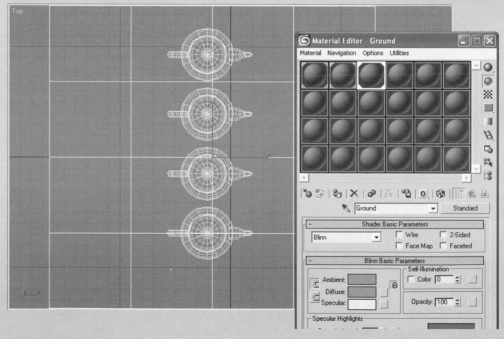

Edit materials.

1. Click the Sample 1 slot (if necessary), then click the 2-Sided check box in the Shader Basic Parameters rollout.

2. Click the Diffuse color swatch in the Blinn Basic Parameters rollout, select the color white in the Color Selector, then click Close.

3. In the Specular Highlights group in the Blinn Basic Parameters rollout, adjust the number in the Specular Level box to **57** and the Glossiness number to **50**.

4. Click the Sample 2 slot, click the 2-Sided check box in the Shader Basic Parameters rollout, click the Diffuse color swatch in the Blinn Basic Parameters rollout, select a dark red color in the Color Selector, then click Close.

5. In the Specular Highlights group in the Blinn Basic Parameters rollout, adjust the number in the Specular Level box to **44**.

6. Switch to the Perspective viewport, then click the Quick Render (Production) tool to render the scene, as shown in Figure 3.

7. Close the rendered scene window, then save the file as **MaterialSamples01**.

FIGURE 3
Rendered scene

Materials and Maps

Understand and assign maps.

1. Select the Ground sample slot, then click the map button to the right of the Diffuse color swatch in the Blinn Basic Parameters rollout.

2. Double-click Checker in the Material/Map Browser, then click the Show Map in Viewport button.

3. In the Coordinates rollout in the Material Editor, change the numbers in the two boxes under Tiling both to **3**, so that the mapped plane looks similar to a checkerboard.

4. Click the Go to Parent button, click the plus sign to the left of Maps in the Material Editor to open the Maps rollout, click and drag the Diffuse map button to the Opacity map button, click the Copy option button in the Copy (Instance) Map dialog box, then click OK.

5. Click the Background button on the Material Editor, click the Opacity map button to open the map's parameters in the Material Editor, change the numbers in the two boxes under Tiling both to **1**, then click the Quick Render (Production) tool to render the scene, as shown in Figure 4.

6. Minimize the rendered scene window, click the Go to Parent button, deselect the check box to the left of Diffuse in the Maps rollout, then render the scene again.

7. Close the rendered scene window, select the check box to the left of Diffuse in the Maps rollout, then save the scene as **MaterialSamples02**.

FIGURE 4
Mapped Diffuse and Opacity components

Navigate materials and maps.

1. In the Material Editor, click the Material/Map Navigator button.

2. Click the Opacity map in the Material/Map Navigator.

3. In the Material Editor, click the map Name field list arrow, then click Ground.

4. Click the Diffuse Color map in the Material/Map Navigator, then click the Go Forward to Sibling button in the Material Editor.

5. In the Material Editor, click the Go to Parent button to show the Ground material in the Material Editor and select it in the Material/Map Navigator, as shown in Figure 5.

6. Click the Opacity map in the Material/Map Navigator, click the map Type button in the Material Editor, then double-click NONE to remove the map from the Opacity component of the material.

7. Close the Material/Map Navigator if desired, then save the file.

FIGURE 5

Material/Map Navigator and Material Editor

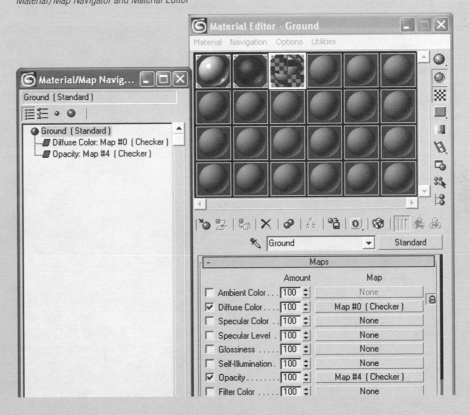

Map basic shader components.

1. Select the Sample 1 slot in the Material Editor, then click the Self-Illumination map button in the Maps rollout.

2. Double-click the Wood map in the Material/Map Browser, change the Grain Thickness for the map to **10**, then render the scene, as shown in Figure 6. If the Wood map is unavailable, choose another map for the Self-Illumination component and adjust its parameters slightly.

3. Minimize the rendered scene window, then click the Go to Parent button.

4. Click and drag the Self-Illumination map button in the Maps rollout to the Opacity map button, click the Swap option button, click OK, then render the scene again.

5. Click and drag the Opacity map button in the Maps rollout to the Diffuse Color map button, click the Swap button, then click OK.

6. Click the Diffuse map button, click the Swap button to swap the two colors in the Wood map, then change the Grain Thickness to **1**.

7. Select the Ground sample slot, then click the Diffuse map button in the Blinn Basic Parameters rollout.

8. Click the Color #1 color swatch, select a navy blue color in the Color Selector, then click Close.

9. Click the Color #2 map button, double-click Noise in the Material/Map Browser, click the Turbulence option button in the Noise Parameters rollout, click the Color #1 color swatch, select a green color in the Color Selector, then click Close. If the Noise map is unavailable, choose another map for Color #2.

10. Render the scene, as shown in Figure 7, then save the file as **MaterialSamples03**.

FIGURE 6
Wood map assigned to Self-Illumination component

FIGURE 7
Noise submap assigned to Checker map

Map other Standard material components.

1. Minimize the rendered scene window, click the map Name field list arrow in the Material Editor, then click Ground.

2. Click the Reflection map button in the Maps rollout, double-click Raytrace in the Material/Map Browser, click the Go to Parent button, then change the number in the Reflection box in the Maps rollout to **40**.

3. Click the Sample 2 slot, click the Reflection map button in the Maps rollout, double-click Raytrace in the Material/Map Browser, click the Go to Parent button, then change the number in the Reflection box in the Maps rollout to **40**.

4. In the Top viewport, create a sphere to the right of the teapots, then in the Perspective viewport, move the sphere so that its base is even with the plane.

5. In the Material Editor, click the sample slot to the right of the Ground sample slot, click the Diffuse map button in the Maps rollout, double-click Noise in the Material/Map Browser, change Color #1 in the Noise map to a dark yellow and Color #2 to a light yellow, then apply the material to the sphere in the scene.

6. Click the Go to Parent button, click the Bump map button in the Maps rollout, then double-click Cellular in the Material/Map Browser.

7. Render the scene, as shown in Figure 8.

8. Save the file as **MaterialSamples04**, then reset 3ds Max.

FIGURE 8
Completed Skills Review

PROJECT BUILDER 1

You work for an animation company that is producing an autumnal scene for a new animated film. You are in charge of creating the look of realistic falling leaves that are blown around by the wind. You have decided to use photo images of real leaves to create the leaf objects in the scene. You scanned a real leaf to create a digital image, then used a graphics program to create the two maps shown in Figure 9. You'll use these maps together to create animatable leaves in 3ds Max.

1. In the Top viewport, create a plane with the dimensions 1440 × 830, zoom out in the Perspective viewport until the entire plane is visible, then save the scene as **FallingLeaf**.

2. Open the Material Editor, select a sample slot, name the sample slot's material **Leaf**, then make the material 2-sided.

3. Click the Diffuse map button, double-click Bitmap in the Material/Map Browser, browse to the drive and directory containing your Data Files, then select Leaf_diffuse.jpg.

4. Apply the Leaf material to the plane in the scene, then show the map in the viewport.

5. Navigate to the Leaf material in the Material Editor, click the Background button, then assign the Leaf_opacity.jpg file from your Data Files folder as a Bitmap to the material's Opacity component.

6. Rotate the plane in the scene until you can see the other side, then render the scene.

7. In the Maps rollout, copy the Diffuse map to the Bump component as an instance, then change the number in the Bump amount box to **-50**.

8. Increase the Leaf material's Specular Level and Glossiness both to **30**.

9. Render the scene again. The leaf should look like that shown in Figure 10.

10. Save the file, then reset 3ds Max.

FIGURE 9
Leaf image files

FIGURE 10
Completed Project Builder 1

You are part of the team building the background for a video game scene in an urban neighborhood of brick townhouses. You need to create an embossed address plate for one of the houses, and plan to use maps rather than modeling to create the embossed look on a flat plane. You want the address plate to appear bolted to a wall, and you also need it to look like it is made of metal that's gotten dirty with age. You decide to use a material provided with 3ds Max to help you create the metal look, and a separate image of the address to create the embossed look.

1. Create a 140×360 plane in the Top viewport.
2. Create a small sphere in one corner of the plane, change its Hemisphere setting to **.7**, then click the Base to Pivot button to create what looks like a bolt on the plane.
3. Make three copies of the sphere, then move each copy to a different corner of the plane, aligning them as necessary for the best look.
4. Open the Material Editor, click the Get Material button, click the Mtl Library option button in the Browse From group in the Material/Map Browser, scroll down, then double-click Metal_Grey_Plain.
5. Rename the sample slot **Bolts**, then apply the Bolts material to each of the spheres.

6. Apply the Metal_Grey_Plain material to a second sample slot, rename it **Plate**, then apply it to the plane.
7. Assign the Address.tif file from your Data Files directory to the Plate material's Bump component.

8. Group the plane and spheres together, rotate the group until it is vertical in the Perspective viewport, then render the scene, as shown in Figure 11.
9. Save the file as **AddressPlate**, then reset 3ds Max.

FIGURE 11
Completed Project Builder 2

PROJECT BUILDER 3

You work for a training firm that has just acquired an eyeglasses manufacturer as a client. The eyeglass designers who work for the company have always designed on paper, but they are ready to take advantage of new technology if it will enable them to work precisely and more efficiently. They are a bit skeptical of learning how to use a 3D design program to accurately create the look of glass, especially glass that realistically refracts light. You will be presenting examples of objects created in 3ds Max to a group of designers from the manufacturer so they can learn what is possible. You decide to use a couple of different examples.

1. Create a box in the Top viewport, then flip its normals so that in the Perspective viewport you can see the base and the back two walls of the box. Save the file as **GlassExamples**.

2. Name the material in a sample slot Walls, color the material light beige, then apply the Walls material to the box.

3. Name the material in a second sample slot Floor, then color the material red.

4. In Polygon subobject level, select the polygon that is the base of the box, then apply the Floor material to the polygon.

5. Create a sphere in the Top viewport, click the Base to Pivot check box so that the sphere's base aligns with the floor of the box, then move the sphere to the back corner of the box.

6. Name a third material **Glass1**, show the colored background in its slot, then color the material a medium blue color.

7. Adjust the Glass1 material's Opacity to **5**, its Specular Level to **90**, and its Glossiness to **50**.

8. Assign the Raytrace map to the Glass1 material's Refraction component.

9. Navigate back to the Glass1 material in the Material Editor, open the Extended Parameters rollout, then change the Index of Refraction to **1.6**.

10. Create a teapot next to the sphere in the box, then deselect the Lid check box in the teapot's Parameters rollout.

11. Apply the Shell modifier to the teapot, then, in the modifier's Parameters rollout, change the Inner Amount to **.5**. The objects in the Perspective viewport should look similar to Figure 12.

FIGURE 12
Sphere and teapot

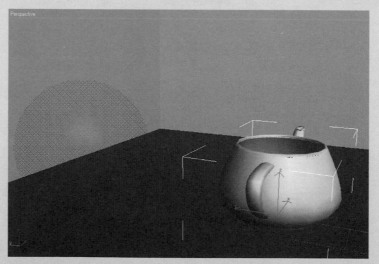

12. Create a new material called **Glass2**, then show the colored background in its slot. Color it light green; change its Opacity to **5**, its Specular Level to **90**, and its Glossiness to **50**; assign the Raytrace map to its Refraction component; then change its Index of Refraction to **1.4**.

13. Apply the Glass2 material to the teapot, then render the scene (it may take a few minutes to completely render). The objects should look similar to those shown in Figure 13.

14. Save the file, then reset 3ds Max.

FIGURE 13
Completed Project Builder 3

DESIGN PROJECT

You work for an advertising agency creating a commercial in which a cartoon spaceship flies through a number of different real-life scenes, weaving between buildings and other elements of each scene, such as trees or people. You have been asked to create the spaceship and an example scene in which it can move behind something in a photo image. You decide to create the spaceship in 3ds Max and use materials other than Standard material to achieve the look that you want.

1. Model a spaceship in a scene, then save the scene as **UFOSighting**.
2. Apply the Ink 'n' Paint material to the spaceship. Adjust the parameters of the material as desired to get the look you want.
3. Click Rendering on the menu bar, click Environment to open the Environment and Effects dialog box, click the Environment map button in the Background group, navigate to the 3dsMax8/maps/ folder containing the maps provided with 3ds Max, then browse through the folders and select a landscape or city scene through which the spaceship could fly.
4. Click Views on the menu bar, click Viewport Background, click the Use Environment Background check box in the Background

group, click the Display Background check box to select it, then click OK.
5. Click Views on the menu bar, click Grids, then click Show Home Grid to deselect it.
6. Choose an object in the background image behind which you want the spaceship to travel, draw a closed spline around the object in the Front viewport, then apply the Extrude modifier to the spline to make it a solid face.

7. Apply the Matte/Shadow material to the spline, then move the spaceship object in the Top viewport so that it is above the spline in the Top viewport.
8. Activate the Front viewport, then render the scene. Adjust the position or rotation of the spaceship to get the look you seek, then render the scene again. An example scene is shown in Figure 14.
9. Save the file, then reset 3ds Max.

FIGURE 14
Example of completed Design Project

PORTFOLIO PROJECT

You work in design for a video game company that is creating a video game version of a popular space battle movie. You are part of a team working on creating the outer space environment that the characters will battle within. Your first task is to create an asteroid field. You'll use materials to create the rocky surfaces of the asteroids and the surfaces of a nearby star and planets.

1. Create three spheres, apply the Noise modifier to each, then separately adjust the Noise modifier parameters for each so that you create three different asteroids.
2. Make several copies of each asteroid and position them within the scene to create a field of asteroids. Re-scale some of the asteroids as necessary so that there are small asteroids and big asteroids in the field.
3. Create at least three different materials simulating a rocky surface and apply each to several asteroids so that all of the asteroids have a rocky surface.
4. Create at least three spheres behind the asteroid field, making one larger than the others.
5. Create a material that simulates a sunlike appearance, then apply it to the largest sphere.
6. Create different materials that simulate the surfaces of planets, then apply each planet material to one of the smaller spheres.
7. Render the scene. An example is shown in Figure 15.
8. Save the file as **Asteroids**, then reset 3ds Max.

FIGURE 15
Example of completed Portfolio Project

chapter

5 CAMERAS AND
LIGHTING

1. Add cameras to a scene.

2. Position cameras.

3. Add lights to a scene.

4. Adjust light parameters.

5. Work with shadows.

6. Use lights.

CHAPTER SUMMARY

In this chapter, you worked with cameras and lights in a scene. You learned what camera objects are and used them to render scenes from different viewpoints. You also created two types of camera objects, target and free, and inserted each into a scene. Later in the chapter, you changed a viewport into a Camera viewport, and worked with a camera using the tools on the Main toolbar. You worked with Safe Frames, which helped you design your scene for TV monitors so that nothing gets cut out. You also added lights to a scene, changed one kind of light into a different kind of light, and made lights cast shadows. You adjusted light parameters, including size, intensity, and color. You also worked with shadows, and assigned a map to a shadow.

FIGURE 1
Scene with lights and shadows

SKILLS REFERENCE

to do this:	use this method:
Adjust a light cone to fit the shape and aspect ratio of a rectangular projected map	Click the Rectangle option button in the Light Cone group in the Spotlight Parameters or Directional Parameters rollout, click the Bitmap Fit button in the Light Cone group, then navigate to and open the file used as the projector map
Adjust the intensity of a light	Adjust the number in the Multiplier box in the Intensity/Color/Attenuation rollout
Adjust the size of a camera's FOV (and focal length)	⊳
Adjust the size of a spot or directional light's falloff	Adjust the number in the Falloff/Field box in the Spotlight Parameters or Directional Parameters rollout
Adjust the size of a spot or directional light's hotspot	Adjust the number in the Hotspot/Beam box in the Spotlight Parameters or Directional Parameters rollout
Adjust the target distance of a free light	Adjust the number in the Targ. Dist. box in the General Parameters rollout
Adjust the target distance of a target light	Move the target without moving the light object **or** Move the light object without moving the target
Blend a light's color with its shadow color in its shadows	Select the Light Affects Shadow Color check box in the Object Shadows group in the Shadow Parameters rollout
Cast shadows with a light	Select the On check box in the Shadows group in the General Parameters rollout

to do this:	use this method:
Change a camera's icon color	Click the color swatch next to the Name text box, select a color in the Object Color dialog box, then click OK
Change a camera's name	Select the text in the Name text box, then type a new name
Change a free light to a target light	Select the Targeted check box in the General Parameters rollout
Change a light cone's shape	Click the Circle option button or Rectangle option button in the Light Cone group in the Spotlight Parameters or Directional Parameters rollout
Change a light type	Select a light, click the Light Type list arrow in the General Parameters rollout, then click Spot, Directional, or Omni
Change a light's icon color	Click the color swatch to the right of the Name text box, click a color in the Object Color dialog box, then click OK
Change a light's name	Select the text in the Name text box, then type a new name
Change a target light to a free light	Deselect the Targeted check box in the General Parameters rollout
Change a viewport to a Camera viewport	Right-click the viewport label, point to Views on the right-click menu, then click the name of the desired camera on the submenu **or** Press [C], then (if necessary) click the name of the desired camera in the Select Camera dialog box and click OK
Change shadow color	Select a light, click the Color color swatch in the Object Shadows group in the Shadow Parameters rollout, choose a color for the shadow, then click Close

to do this:	use this method:
Change shadow density	Adjust the number in the Dens. box in the Shadow Parameters rollout
Change the color emitted by a light	Click the color swatch to the right of the Multiplier box in the Intensity/Color/Attenuation rollout, choose a color, then click Close
Create a free camera	Click 📷 on the Create panel, click the Free button in the Object Type rollout, then click in the viewport where you want the camera to be
Create a free directional light	Click 🔦 on the Create panel, click the Free Direct button in the Object Type rollout, then click in a viewport to set the light's location
Create a free spotlight	Click 🔦 on the Create panel, click the Free Spot button in the Object Type rollout, then click in a viewport to set the light's location
Create a target camera (with a target object)	Click 📷 on the Create panel, click the Target button in the Object Type rollout, click in the viewport where you want the camera to be, drag to the location of the target object, then release the mouse button
Create a target directional light	Click 🔦 on the Create panel, click the Target Direct button in the Object Type rollout, click in the viewport to set the light's location, drag to another location in the viewport, then release the mouse button to set the location of the target
Create a target spotlight	Click 🔦 on the Create panel, click the Target Spot button in the Object Type rollout, click in the viewport to set the light's location, drag to another location in the viewport, then release the mouse button to set the location of the target

to do this:	use this method:
Create an omni light	Click ✎ on the Create panel, click the Omni button in the Object Type rollout, then click in a viewport to set the light's location
Decay a light based on the distance of a lit surface from the light source or near attenuation End point	Click the Type list arrow in the Decay group in the Intensity/Color/Attenuation rollout, then click Inverse
Decay a light as it would actually decay in a real-world situation	Click the Type list arrow in the Decay group in the Intensity/Color/Attenuation rollout, then click Inverse Square
Decay a light from a set start point	Adjust the number in the Start box in the Decay group in the Intensity/Color/Attenuation rollout
Dolly a camera	⌖
Dolly a camera and its target at the same time	⌖
Dolly a camera toward or away from objects in a scene and affect the distortion of the objects	◈
Dolly a target	⌖

to do this:	use this method:
Engulf an entire scene in bright light	Select the Overshoot check box to the right of the Show Cone check box in the Light Cone group
Increase or decrease the field-of-view (FOV) of a camera	Increase or decrease the number of degrees in the FOV box in the Parameters rollout **or** Decrease or increase the number of millimeters in the Lens box in the Parameters rollout **or** Click a button in the Stock Lenses group in the Parameters rollout
Increase or decrease the focal length of a camera	Increase or decrease the number of millimeters in the Lens box in the Parameters rollout **or** Decrease or increase the number of degrees in the FOV box in the Parameters rollout **or** Click a button in the Stock Lenses group in the Parameters rollout
Light only the ambient component of a surface	Select the Ambient Only check box in the Advanced Effects rollout
Light only the diffuse component of a surface	Select the Diffuse check box in the Advanced Effects rollout and deselect the Specular check box
Light only the specular component of a surface	Select the Specular check box in the Advanced Effects rollout and deselect the Diffuse check box
Make a spot or directional light's cone visible at all times	Click the Show Cone check box in the Light Cone group of the Spotlight Parameters or Directional Parameters rollout

to do this:	use this method:
Map a shadow	Click the Map check box in the Object Shadows group in the Shadow Parameters rollout, click the map button next to the check box, click a map in the Material/Map Browser, then click OK
Move a camera through a scene as though walking through the scene	⚇
Move a camera's position parallel to the Camera viewport's view	✋
Project a map with a light	Select the Map check box in the Projector Map group on the Advanced Effects rollout, click the map button next to the check box, click Bitmap in the Material/Map Browser, then navigate to and open the file to be projected
Rotate a camera around its axis while keeping it aimed in the same direction	↻
Rotate a free camera around its own axes	⇥
Rotate a free camera around the plane at the end of its FOV cone	⬭
Rotate a target around its target camera	⇥
Rotate a target camera around its target	⬭

to do this:	use this method:
Show a camera's FOV cone whether or not it is selected	Select the camera, then select the Show Cone check box in the Parameters rollout
Show attenuation indicators in the viewports	Click the Show check box in the Near Attenuation and/or Far Attenuation groups in the Intensity/Color/Attenuation rollout
Show the decay indicator in the light's cone	Click the Show check box in the Decay group in the Intensity/Color/Attenuation rollout
Turn on Safe Frames	Right-click the active viewport name, then click Show Safe Frames
Use far attenuation	Select the Use check box in the Far Attenuation group in the Intensity/Color/Attenuation rollout, adjust the number in the Start box, then adjust the number in the End box
Use near attenuation	Select the Use check box in the Near Attenuation group in the Intensity/Color/Attenuation rollout, adjust the number in the Start box, then adjust the number in the End box

Add cameras to a scene.

1. Open MAXWB05-01.max from the drive and directory where your Data Files are stored, then adjust the view in the Top viewport so that you can see the box on the table, the table, and the entire floor of the room the table is in.

2. Click the Create tab (if necessary), click the Cameras button on the Create panel, then click the Target button in the Object Type rollout.

3. In the Top viewport, click and drag from the lower left corner of the room to the box on the table, then release the mouse button.

4. Click the Free button in the Object Type rollout, then click on the box in the Top viewport to insert a free camera.

5. Select the target camera, click the Modify tab, click the Show Cone check box in the Parameters rollout, then change the FOV for the camera to **30**.

6. Select the free camera, then click the Show Cone check box in the Parameters rollout. The cameras should look like those shown in Figure 2.

7. Save the file as **BoxTable01**.

FIGURE 2

Cameras added to scene

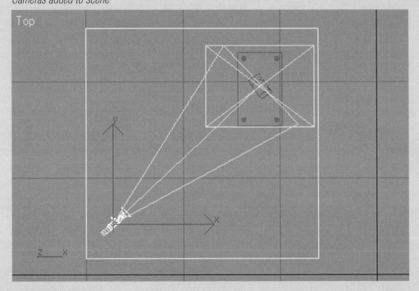

Position cameras.

1. Select Camera02 in the Front viewport, deselect the Show Cone check box in the Parameters rollout, move the camera up so that it is even with the top of the wall behind it, then deselect Camera02.

2. Activate the Left viewport, then press [F3] to change the viewport to Smooth + Highlights.

3. Press [C], click Camera01 in the Select Camera dialog box, then click OK.

4. Right-click the Camera viewport label, then click Show Safe Frame.

5. In the Front viewport, move Camera01 up so that it is about two thirds of the way up the wall behind it in the scene, then move Camera01's target up so that is in the center of the box.

6. Click the 24mm button in the Parameters rollout for Camera01.

7. Click in the Camera viewport, click the Dolly Camera button, drag up in the Camera viewport to move the camera closer to the box, click the Pan Camera button, then drag in the viewport (if necessary) until the viewport looks like Figure 3.

8. Save the file.

FIGURE 3
Camera viewport with Safe Frames

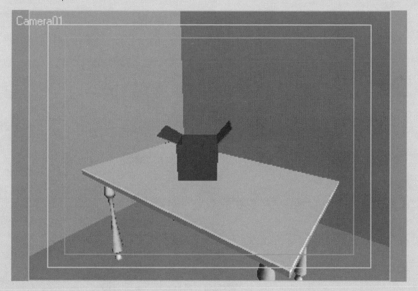

Add lights to a scene.

1. Click the Create tab, click the Lights button on the Create panel, then click Free Spot in the Object Type rollout.
2. Click in the upper left corner of the room in the Top viewport to insert the spotlight, then in the Front viewport, move the light up until it is close to or even with the top of the wall behind it.
3. In the Top viewport, move the light so that it is even with the top center of the table, as shown in Figure 4.
4. Click the Light Type list arrow in the General Parameters rollout, click Directional, then click the On check box in the Shadows group.
5. Save the file as **BoxTable02**.

FIGURE 4
Light inserted in scene

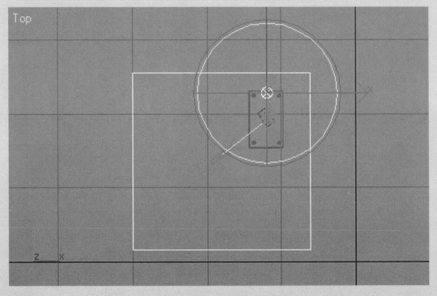

Adjust light parameters.

1. In the Directional Parameters rollout, change the Hotspot/Beam to **5** and the Falloff/Field to **5.5**, then render the Camera viewport, as shown in Figure 5.

2. Minimize the rendered scene window, then deselect the On check box in the Light Type group in the General Parameters rollout to turn the directional light off.

3. Click the Create tab, click the Omni button in the Object Type rollout on the Lights panel, then click in the upper left corner of the room in the Top viewport.

4. In the Front viewport, move the omni light so that it is close to or even with the top of the wall behind it.

5. Back in the Top viewport, press and hold [Shift] while moving the Omni01 light, click the Instance option button, change the Number of Copies to **5**, then arrange the light instances, as shown in Figure 6, in the Top viewport.

6. Select one of the omni lights, then click the On check box in the Shadows group of the General Parameters rollout.

7. Click the Modify tab, then change the Multiplier number in the Intensity/Color/Attenuation rollout to **.2**.

8. Save the file.

FIGURE 5

Light with hotspot and falloff adjusted

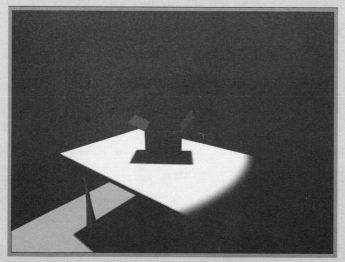

FIGURE 6

Instances of omni light

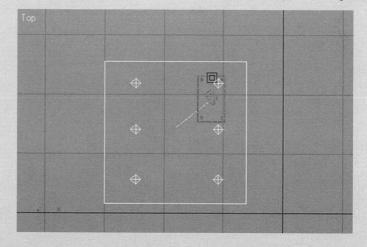

Cameras and Lighting

Work with shadows.

1. In the Shadow Parameters rollout, change the Dens. to **.75**.

2. Click the Map map button in the Shadow Parameters rollout, then double-click Dent in the Material/Map Browser.

3. Render the scene, as shown in Figure 7.

4. Minimize the rendered scene window, deselect the Map check box in the Shadow Parameters rollout, then render the scene again.

5. Save the file as **BoxTable03**.

FIGURE 7

Mapped shadows cast by omni lights

Use lights.

1. Delete the box on top of the table from the scene.

2. Select one of the omni lights, then change its Multiplier to **.1** in the Intensity/Color/Attenuation rollout.

3. Select the directional light, then select the On check box in the Light Type group to turn it on.

4. Move the directional light in the Top viewport until it is over the center of the table.

5. In the Advanced Effects rollout for the light, click the map button next to the Map check box in the Projector Map group, double-click Bitmap in the Material/Map Browser, navigate to the 3dsMax8/maps/Metal folder, click GALVPLAT, then click Open.

6. Open the Directional Parameters rollout, click the Rectangle option button in the Light Cone group, click the Bitmap Fit button beneath the Rectangle option button, navigate to 3dsMax8/maps/Metal, click GALVPLAT, then click Open.

7. Click in the Camera viewport, then render the scene, as shown in Figure 8.

8. Save the file as **BoxTable04**, then reset 3ds Max.

FIGURE 8
Map projected by light onto table

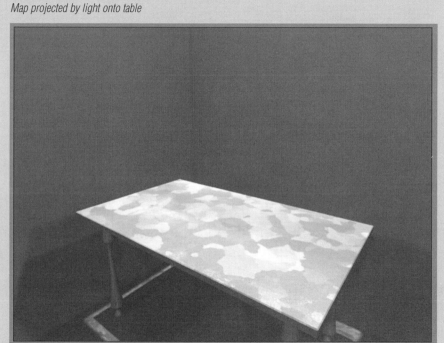

You work for an architect creating digital images of planned projects. The architect has a client who wants to see a visual of a planned room lit by a table lamp in the room, and the architect has asked you to create the visual. You have already built the room, which contains a table and a lamp. You need to apply appropriate materials to the lamp, make the lamp a light source, and add other lighting to the room that lights the areas unaffected by the lamp. You also plan to use a camera to control the point from which the room is viewed.

1. Open MAXWB05-02.max from the drive and directory where your Data Files are stored.
2. Open the Material Editor, rename the 04-Default material **Lamp**, recolor the material's Diffuse component, increase its Specular Level and Glossiness so that the material has a shiny look, then apply the material to the lamp base in the scene.
3. Rename the 05-Default material **Lampshade**, recolor the material's Diffuse component to a yellow shade, increase the Self-Illumination value for the material to **50** so that it appears to be lit from within, then apply the material to the lampshade in the scene.
4. Click the Lights button on the Create panel, click the Omni button in the Object Type

rollout, click in the center of the lamp in the Top viewport to insert an omni light, then move the omni light up in the Front viewport until it is located where a lightbulb in the lamp would be.

5. Click the Shadows On check box for the omni light, then make sure that the light's intensity multiplier is at **1** in the Intensity/Color/Attenuation rollout.
6. Click the Cameras button on the Create panel, click the Target button in the Object

Type rollout, click in the center left of the Top viewport, drag to the lamp, then release the mouse button.

7. Convert the Left viewport into a Camera viewport, turn on Safe Frames, convert the viewport to Smooth + Highlights, then reposition the camera and target and otherwise adjust the camera view so that the target is in the center of the lamp base and the Camera viewport looks like Figure 9.

FIGURE 9
Camera viewport

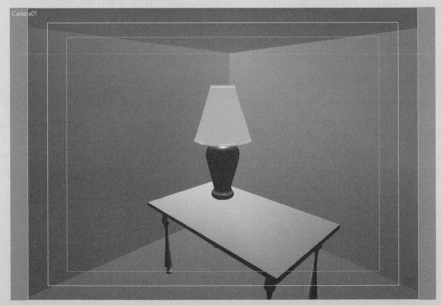

8. Click the Lights button on the Create panel, click the Omni button in the Object Type rollout, click in the upper left corner of the room in the Top viewport to insert an omni light, then move the light up in the Front viewport so that the top of the light object is even with the room's ceiling.

9. Instance the new omni light in the Top viewport to create five copies of it, arrange the lights in three rows of two across the top of the room, then reduce the Multiplier for the lights to **.1**.

10. Select the table, lamp, lamp light, and lampshade, and move them so that the table is against the wall; then move the lamp, light, and shade so that they are up next to the wall.

11. Open the Material Editor, then increase the Self-Illumination value of the Lampshade material to **80**.

12. Select the omni light in the lamp, open the Shadow Map Params rollout, then change the Sample Range value to **20** to soften the shadows cast by the light.

13. Reposition the camera so that it is aimed at the lamp and table from the opposite corner of the room, then render the Camera viewport, as shown in Figure 10.

14. Save the file as **LampRoom**, then reset 3ds Max.

FIGURE 10
Completed Project Builder 1

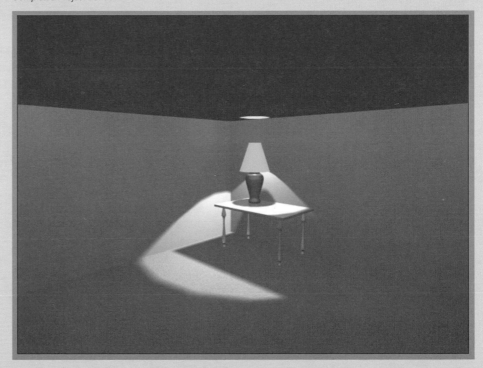

PROJECT BUILDER 2

You work for an advertising agency creating a commercial for a battery company. You have already created a flashlight that will be animated in the commercial, and have applied appropriate materials to its components. Now you need to give the flashlight a light beam. You also need to set up appropriate lighting of the flashlight itself and create a camera angle of the flashlight that can be animated.

1. Open MAXWB05-03.max from the drive and directory where your Data Files are stored.

2. Zoom out in the Front viewport, then insert a target spotlight well above the flashlight, creating its target below the flashlight in the viewport so that the light is aimed at the flashlight.

3. Insert a target camera in the scene, change the Perspective viewport to a Camera viewport, show Safe Frames in the camera viewport, then adjust the camera view so that you can see the entire flashlight within the title safe frame as well as an area on the left where the flashlight's beam will be visible, as shown in Figure 11.

4. Select the spotlight, turn shadows on for the light, change the density of the light's shadows to .75, then open the Shadow Map Params rollout and change the Sample Range number to **10** to soften its shadows.

5. Decrease the size of the hotspot of the spotlight so that it is only slightly bigger than the flashlight, then increase the size of falloff slightly, as shown in Figure 12.

6. Insert a free spotlight in the Left viewport, then rotate it 180 degrees in the Top viewport so that it is aimed out of the flashlight.

FIGURE 11
Camera view of flashlight

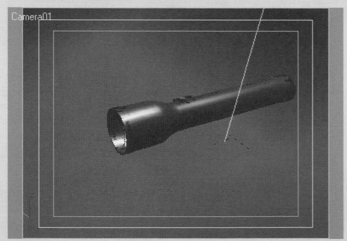

FIGURE 12
Hotspot and falloff of spotlight adjusted

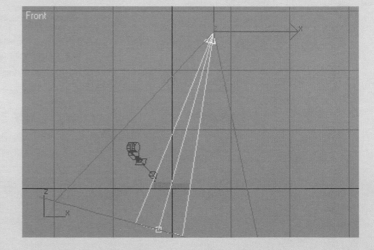

7. Delete the sphere that is at the base of the half-sphere within the top of the flashlight, position the new spotlight at the base of the half-sphere, then rotate the light slightly to match the angle in which the flashlight is aimed.

8. Click the Use and Show check boxes in the Near Attenuation group in the light's Intensity/Color/Attenuation rollout, then adjust the Near Attenuation Start value to about **75**.

9. Increase the light's hotspot to be close in value to its falloff, then move the light object back a little further in the flashlight until the light's cone exits the flashlight right at its edges.

10. Turn the light's shadows on, then increase the Sample Range value in the Shadow Map Params rollout to **30**.

11. Tint the light a yellow color, increase its Multiplier to **5**, then render the Camera viewport, as shown in Figure 13.

12. Save the file as **FlashlightOn**, then reset 3ds Max.

FIGURE 13
Completed Project Builder 2

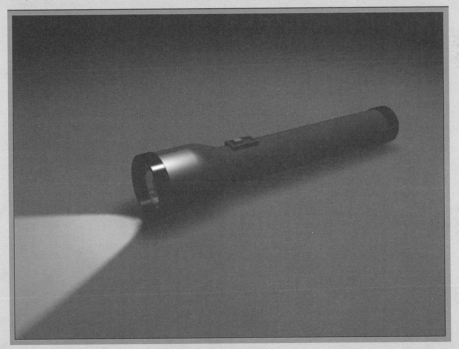

As a level designer for a new video game based in a metropolis, you are creating a city environment in which the characters of the new game will interact. You need to create appropriate lighting for the streets in the environment, and you plan to create both a night setting and a day setting using the same lights. You also want to create a few different camera views in the scene to get different angles on the characters as they move around the city.

1. Open MAXWB05-04.max from the drive and directory where your Data Files are stored.
2. Insert a free spotlight into the scene, position it within the streetlamp so that it faces down onto the street, then increase its intensity Multiplier to **2**.
3. Link the light to the streetlamp, then make two instances of the lamp and light, and position each near a trash can on the sidewalk.
4. Make multiple instances of the streetlamps and light objects, position them on the other street sidewalks in the scene, then copy multiple trash cans and position them near the streetlamps on the sidewalks.
5. Zoom out in the Front viewport; insert a target directional light in the top of the viewport aimed at the city, with its target located under the city; increase the size of

the light's hotspot so that the entire city scene is encompassed by it; then increase its Multiplier to **1.5**.
6. Insert two cameras into the scene in two different locations: one (Camera01) looking down the length of the two blocks of buildings, and one (Camera02) aimed down the

short street between the two blocks of buildings.
7. Create Camera viewports for each camera; adjust the view of Camera01 to an interesting angle; render the scene to show the city with nighttime lighting, as shown in Figure 14; then save the file as **CityNightCam1**.

FIGURE 14
Nighttime city lighting

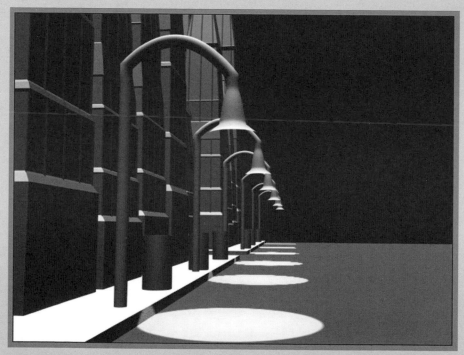

8. Turn on shadows for the directional light, increase the density of its shadows to **1.5**, increase its Multiplier to **2.5**, then turn off the streetlamp spotlights.

9. Adjust the view of Camera02 to an interesting angle; render the scene to show the city with daytime lighting, as shown in Figure 15; then save the file as **CityDayCam2**.

10. Reset 3ds Max.

FIGURE 15
Daytime city lighting

DESIGN PROJECT

You are an industrial designer working for a light manufacturer. You are responsible for coming up with a new type of chandelier for this year's line. You have decided to go with a wrought iron look and to avoid using straight lines in the light. You are using 3ds Max to model the chandelier and to demonstrate how lights look within it.

1. Create splines in the shapes appropriate for a chandelier, then create loft objects using the splines and a small rectangle to create the look of wrought iron.

2. Apply the Mirror modifier to the splines to create mirror images, then reposition the loft objects to create a symmetrical chandelier.

3. Create splines and apply the Lathe modifier to them in order to create the glass containers for the light bulbs in the chandelier, and bases for the containers (i.e., where they are attached to the wrought iron).

4. Model the beginning of the chain that is attached to the chandelier.

5. Insert a camera in the scene, convert a viewport into a Camera viewport with Safe Frames, then adjust the view of the chandelier so that all the key parts are within the action safe frame.

6. Create and apply materials to the chandelier components to create an appropriate look for the iron parts, the glass light containers, and so on. Render the camera view as you work to make sure the fixture looks the way you want.

7. Create and instance a light, position the instances in the light containers of the chandelier, then adjust the parameters of the lights as necessary to get the look you want.

8. Create lighting separate from the chandelier that lights the chandelier for the purposes of demonstrating its nice appearance to the executives at the light manufacturer. Turn shadows on or off as necessary to create the most appealing environment for the light fixture.

9. When complete, render the camera view again, then save the file as **Chandelier**. An example of what you might create is shown in Figure 16.

10. Reset 3ds Max.

FIGURE 16

Example of completed Design Project

PORTFOLIO PROJECT

You work in design at a marketing company and are creating a postcard to be sent to potential attendees of a business strategy seminar. The company running the seminar is using chess as the theme in its marketing, to focus on the importance of strategic thinking. They want a sophisticated look for the postcard and you have decided to use 3ds Max to achieve this goal.

1. Create a chess piece or pieces using a spline and the Lathe modifier, then create a surface for the piece to be resting on.
2. Create and apply materials to the chess piece and the surface, so that the piece is shiny and realistically reflects its surroundings, and so that the surface it is resting on looks like a sophisticated chessboard.
3. Create lighting in the scene that highlights the chess piece but also shows a good portion of the surrounding chessboard. Again, keep in mind that you are going for a sophisticated look.
4. Adjust the chess piece material as necessary once you've created the scene lighting to create the most realistic look possible for the piece.
5. Insert a camera in the scene, convert a viewport into a Camera viewport, show Safe

Frames, and adjust the camera view so that the image you want to appear on the postcard is within the action safe frame.
6. Render the Camera viewport. An example of what the scene might look like is shown in Figure 17.
7. Save the file as **Strategy**, then reset 3ds Max.

FIGURE 17
Example of completed Portfolio Project

chapter

6 ANIMATION

1. Animate with Auto Key.

2. Animate with Set Key.

3. Configure animation timing.

4. Edit keys.

5. Use the Dope Sheet.

6. Use the Curve Editor.

7. Assign animation controllers.

8. Assign animation constraints.

CHAPTER SUMMARY

In this chapter, you animated scenes using Auto Key, and you practiced animating different kinds of objects and parameters. You animated objects using Set Key mode, and you filtered the parameters for which keyframes are set. You adjusted animation frame rates, defined the length and re-scaled the timing of an animation, and edited the playback properties of an animation. You selected, moved, deleted, and cloned keys on the track bar and edited the properties for single key values. You used Track View's Dope Sheet to adjust individual keyframes and parent-child keyframes. You also used the Curve Editor to modify animation timing, values, and motion, and to add keys to an animation. You learned about the role of animation controllers in 3ds Max animation and assigned controllers to animation tracks. You learned how animation constraints operate, assigned constraints, and adjusted the parameters and options within a constraint. Lastly, you used a List controller to assign multiple controllers to an animation track at the same time.

FIGURE 1
Animated scene

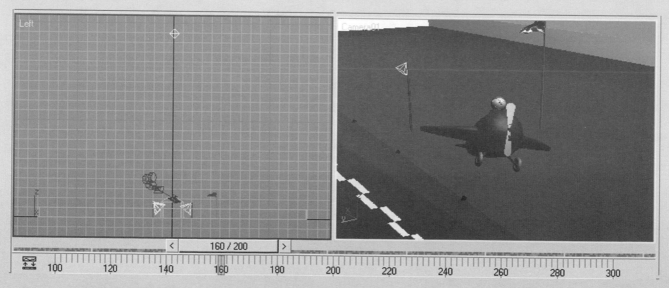

SKILLS REFERENCE

to do this:	use this method:
Add a key to the function curve in the Curve Editor	Click ⚡ in the Curve Editor, then click anywhere on the curve to insert the key
Adjust the speed at which an animation is played	Click the 1/4x, 1/2x, 1x, 2x, or 4x option button in the Time Configuration dialog box, then click OK
Animate an object using Auto Key	Turn on Auto Key, move the time slider from the 0 frame to a later frame, then select and change the object parameter(s)
Animate an object using Set Key	Turn on Set Key, move the time slider (if necessary) to the appropriate starting frame, change the object's parameter(s), click ⚿ , move the slider to another frame, change the object's parameter(s), then click ⚿ again
Assign a new controller to a List controller	Select the Available controller under the List controller in the Assign Controller list on the Motion panel, click 🔲 , select a controller from the list, then click OK
Assign an animation constraint to a selected object	Click Animation on the menu bar, point to Constraints, click the constraint on the submenu, then click the object to which you want the selected object to be constrained **or** Click 🔘 , click the desired track in the list in the Assign Controller rollout, click 🔲 , select a constraint from the list, click OK, then add the target or path using the constraint's rollout on the Motion panel
Assign an animation controller to a selected object's transform tracks	Click Animation on the menu bar, point to Transform Controllers, Position Controllers, Rotation Controllers, or Scale Controllers, then click a controller on the submenu

to do this:	use this method:
Assign an animation controller to a selected track	Click (icon), click the desired track in the list in the Assign Controller rollout, click (icon), select a controller from the list, then click OK **or** Open Track View, right-click the track to which you want to assign the controller, select Assign Controller from the Quad menu, then select a controller from the list
Change a keyed value	Adjust the number in the Value box in the Key Info dialog box **or** Click (icon) in the Curve Editor, then click and drag the key up or down
Change an In or Out tangent to a Custom tangent (enables manual adjustment using tangent handles)	
Change an In or Out tangent to a Fast tangent (speeds up the object near the key)	
Change an In or Out tangent to a Flat tangent (curved interpolation, no overshoot)	
Change an In or Out tangent to a Linear tangent (straight line interpolation)	

to do this:	use this method:
Change an In or Out tangent to a Slow tangent (slows down the object near the key)	
Change an In or Out tangent to a Smooth tangent (curved interpolation)	
Change an In or Out tangent to a Step tangent (holds a value constant from one key to the next, then switches)	
Change how time is displayed in an animation	Click the Frames, SMPTE, FRAME:TICKS, or MM:SS:TICKS option button in the Time Configuration dialog box, then click OK
Change the frame rate of an animation to a custom rate	Click the Custom option button in the Time Configuration dialog box, enter the frame rate in the FPS box, then click OK
Change the frame rate of an animation to a standard rate	Click the NTSC, PAL, or Film option button in the Time Configuration dialog box, then click OK
Change the length of an animation's active time segment	Change the number in the Start and/or End Time boxes in the Time Configuration dialog box, then click OK **or** Change the number in the Length box in the Time Configuration dialog box, then click OK

to do this:	use this method:
Clone a key or keys	Press and hold [Shift], then click and drag the key or keys to a new location
Copy the In tangent type to the previous or next Out tangent	Click ← or → next to the In tangent flyout
Copy the Out tangent type to the previous or next In tangent	Click ← or → next to the Out tangent flyout
Delete a key	Select the key, then press [Delete] **or** Right-click the key, point to Delete Key, then click the name of the key (checked) on the submenu
Delete a keyed value from a keyframe	Right-click the key, point to Delete Key, then click the value to be deleted on the submenu
Display a selection range bar beneath the timeline	Right-click the track bar, point to Configure, then click Show Selection Range
Display an object's trajectory	Right-click an animated object, click Properties, click the Trajectory check box in the Object Properties dialog box, then click OK
Filter a keyframe in Set Key mode	Move the time slider to the desired frame, click the Key Filters button on the status bar, select the check box(es) in the Set Key Filters dialog box for those parameters to be keyed, close the dialog box, make changes to the object, and then click ⊶
Keyframe all parameters in Set Key mode	Move the time slider to the desired frame, click the Key Filters button on the status bar, click the All check box in the Set Key Filters dialog box, close the dialog box, make changes to the object, then click ⊶

to do this:	use this method:
Move a key and all of its child keys to a different frame	In the Dope Sheet, click and drag the parent key to a new location
Move a key or keys to a different frame or frames	Click and drag the key(s) to a new location on the track bar **or** Click and drag the key(s) to a new location in the Dope Sheet **or** Click ⊹ in the Curve Editor, then click and drag the key(s) left or right **or** Click ⟨⊹⟩ in the Curve Editor, then click and drag the key(s) left or right
Move a keyed value to a new location	Change the number in the Time box in the key's properties dialog box
Move between keys	Click the arrow buttons in the upper left corner of the key's properties dialog box
Open the Curve Editor	▦ **or** Click Graph Editors on the menu bar, then click Track View-Curve Editor **or** Right-click an object, then click Curve Editor on the Transform menu
Open the Dope Sheet	Click Graph Editors on the menu bar, then click Track View-Dope Sheet **or** Right-click an object, then click Dope Sheet on the Transform menu
Open the Mini Curve Editor	⧮
Open the Time Configuration dialog box	▤

to do this:	use this method:
Play an animation	Move the time slider from left to right or ▶️
Play an animation back in all viewports	Deselect the Active Viewport Only check box in the Time Configuration dialog box, click OK, then click ▶️
Play an animation forward, then in reverse, then forward, then in reverse, and so on	Move the time slider from left to right, then right to left, and so on or Deselect the Real Time check box in the Time Configuration dialog box, click the Ping-Pong option button, click OK, then click ▶️
Play an animation in reverse	Move the time slider from right to left or Deselect the Real Time check box in the Time Configuration dialog box, click the Reverse option button, click OK, then click ▶️
Play an animation once only	Deselect the Loop check box in the Time Configuration dialog box, click OK, then click ▶️
Re-scale animation timing	Click the Re-scale Time button in the Time Configuration dialog box, change the numbers in the appropriate boxes to change the length of the active time segment, then click OK or Select the keys to be re-scaled, show the selection range bar underneath the timeline, then click and drag a square on one end of the bar
Scale a key value or values up or down	Click ⬜ in the Curve Editor, then click and drag the key(s) up or down
Scale the placement in time of a key or keys	Click ⬜ in the Curve Editor, then click and drag the key(s) left or right

to do this:	use this method:
Select a key	Make sure the appropriate object is selected, then click the key on the track bar
Select multiple keys at the same time	Click and drag on the track bar to create a selection region around multiple keys, then release the mouse button
Show all frames in an animation during playback	Deselect the Real Time check box in the Time Configuration dialog box, click OK, then click ▶
Stop an animation	▮▮
Turn on Auto Key	Click the Toggle Auto Key Mode button on the status bar
Turn on Set Key	Click the Toggle Set Key Mode button on the status bar
View a specific frame in an animation	Move the time slider to the frame number on the timeline or Enter the frame number in the Current Frame (Go To Frame) box on the status bar or Enter the frame number in the Current Time box in the Time Configuration dialog box, then click OK
View the animation timeline and keyframes of an object	Select the object
View the properties for a key value in the Key Info dialog box	Right-click the key on the track bar, then click the key value on the submenu or Right-click the key in the Dope Sheet or the Curve Editor

Animate with Auto Key.

1. Open the file MAXWB06-01.max from the drive and directory containing your Data Files.

2. In the Top viewport, create a teapot just below the light; create a new material in the Material Editor with a light brown Diffuse color, Specular Level of **50**, and Glossiness of **40**; then apply the material to the teapot.

3. Switch to the Front viewport, zoom in on the scene, click the Toggle Auto Key Mode button on the status bar, move the time slider to frame 40, then move the teapot up and to the left in the viewport.

4. Move the time slider to frame 60, move the teapot down along its z-axis, move the time slider to frame 80, move the teapot to the right along its x-axis, move the time slider to 90, then move the teapot up and to the left again.

5. Move the time slider to 100, then move the teapot down and to the right so that it is centered between the eyes.

6. Click the Toggle Auto Key Mode button to turn Auto Key off, right-click the teapot, click Properties, click the Trajectory check box in the Display Properties group in the Object Properties dialog box, then click OK. The trajectory for the teapot should look similar to Figure 2.

FIGURE 2

Teapot's trajectory during animation

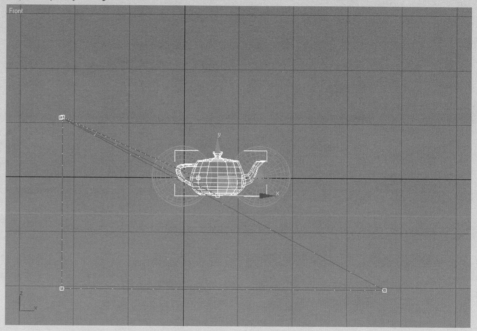

7. Move the time slider back to frame 0, select the light in the scene, click the Modify tab, open the Intensity/Color/Attenuation rollout, then change the Multiplier to **0**.

8. Click the Toggle Auto Key Mode button to turn Auto Key on, move the time slider to frame 20, change the light's Multiplier to **1**, then click the Toggle Auto Key Mode button to turn off Auto Key.

9. Switch to the Perspective viewport, play the animation, then stop the animation.

10. Move the time slider to frame 10, then render the scene. Because the light is only at a .5 multiplier in frame 10, your scene should look like Figure 3.

11. Minimize the rendered scene window, then save the file as **Eyes01**.

FIGURE 3
Animation at frame 10

Animate with Set Key.

1. Move the time slider to frame 0; click the Key Filters button; deselect the Position, Scale, and IK Parameters check boxes in the Set Key Filters dialog box so that only the Rotation check box is selected; then close the Set Key Filters dialog box.

2. Click the Toggle Set Key Mode button, click the Set Keys button, move the time slider to frame 30, rotate the teapot 90 degrees around its x-axis, then click the Set Keys button again.

3. Move the time slider to frame 50, rotate the teapot –90 degrees around its z-axis, click the Set Keys button, move the time slider to frame 70, rotate the teapot in any direction you want, click the Set Keys button, move the time slider to frame 85, rotate the teapot in a different direction again, then click the Set Keys button.

4. Move the time slider to frame 100; right-click the Select and Rotate tool; enter **0** in each of the X, Y, and Z boxes in the Absolute:World group in the Rotate Transform Type-In dialog box; then close the Transform Type-In dialog box.

5. Click the Set Keys button, then click the Toggle Set Key Mode button to turn off Set Key.

6. Play the animation, then stop the animation after you have viewed it a few times.

7. Move the time slider to frame 40. The scene at this point should look similar to Figure 4.

8. Save the file as **Eyes02**.

FIGURE 4
Animation at frame 40

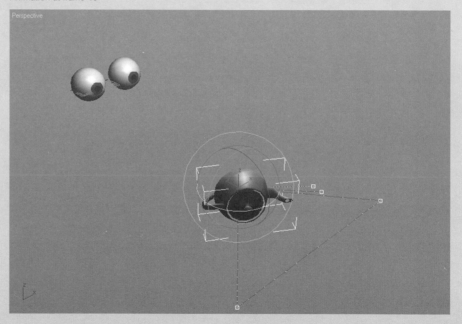

Configure animation timing.

1. Click the Time Configuration button; click the Re-Scale Time button in the Animation group in the Time Configuration dialog box; change the End Time to **150** in the New group in the Re-Scale Time dialog box; then click OK.
2. Click the FRAME:TICKS option button in the Time Display group in the Time Configuration dialog box, deselect the Real Time check box in the Playback group, click the Ping Pong option button in the Playback group, then click OK.
3. Select the teapot if it is not already selected, move the time slider to frame 80, then compare the time display, active time segment length, and keys for the teapot to those shown in Figure 5.
4. Play the animation, then stop the animation after viewing it a few times.
5. Save the file as **Eyes03**.

FIGURE 5
Scene with time re-scaled and time display changed

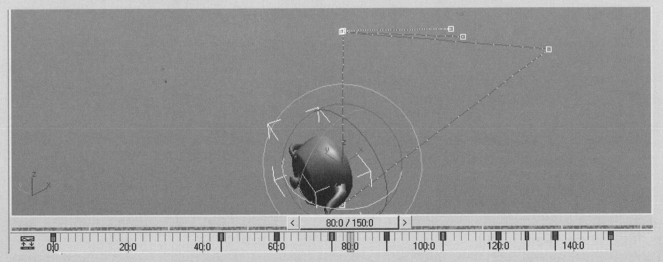

Edit keys.

1. Select the light, click its key at frame 30, then drag the key to frame 20 so that the light reaches a multiplier of 1 earlier in the animation.

2. Select the key at frame 0, press and hold [Shift], then click and drag the key to frame 150 so that the light's multiplier is 0 at the end of the animation.

3. Click the Time Configuration button, click the Real Time check box in the Playback group in the Time Configuration dialog box, then click OK.

4. Play the animation, then stop the animation after viewing it a couple of times.

5. Select the key at frame 20, press and hold [Shift], then click and drag the key to frame 140. The light stays at a multiplier of 1 from frame 20 to frame 140, then turns off by frame 150.

6. Select the teapot, right-click the rotation key at frame 105, point to Delete Key on the right-click menu, then click Teapot01: Rotation on the submenu to delete the key.

7. Right-click the key at frame 120, then click Teapot01: Z Position on the right-click menu.

8. In the Key Info dialog box, change the number in the Value box to **0**, then press [Enter]. The scene should look like Figure 6.

9. Close the Key Info dialog box, play the animation a few times, stop the animation, then save the file as **Eyes04**.

FIGURE 6

Value changed for teapot's Z Position key

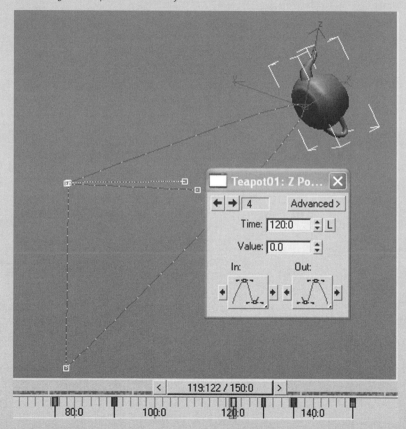

Use the Dope Sheet.

1. Click Graph Editors on the menu bar, then click Track View – Dope Sheet to open the Dope Sheet.

2. Expand the size of the Dope Sheet window and pan down in the Controller window (if necessary) until you see Teapot01, then click the plus sign to the left of Teapot01.

3. Click the plus sign next to Transform under the Teapot01 heading, then click the plus sign next to Rotation under the Transform heading.

4. Select the Z Rotation key at frame 75, then drag it to frame 65.

5. Select the Teapot01 key at frame 120, then drag it to frame 110. The Dope Sheet should now resemble Figure 7.

6. Close the Dope Sheet, then move the time slider to frame 110. The scene and status bar should look similar to Figure 8.

7. Save the file as **Eyes05**.

FIGURE 7
Dope Sheet after keys are moved

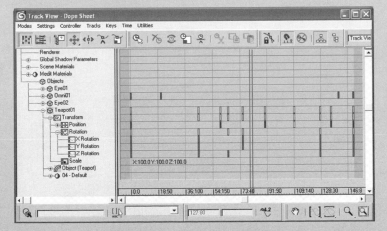

FIGURE 8
Scene at frame 110 after keys are moved

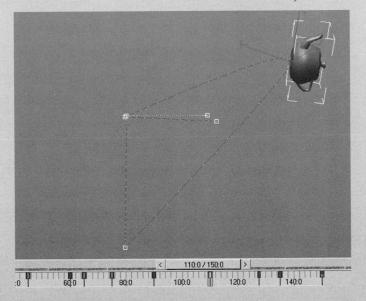

Use the Curve Editor.

1. Click Graph Editors on the menu bar, then click Track View – Curve Editor to open the Curve Editor.

2. Expand the Curve Editor and pan down in the Controller window until you see Teapot01 and its tracks; click the Z Position track; press [Ctrl]; then click the X Position track so that the curves for both tracks show in the Curve Editor, similar to the tracks shown in Figure 9.

3. Select the X Position key at frame 110, then move it so that its value is 100 without moving it to a different frame.

4. Click the Add Keys button on the Curve Editor toolbar, click the Z Position curve at the midpoint between its second and third keys to add a key there, click the Move Keys button on the Curve Editor toolbar, then move the new key so that its value is 0 at frame 77.

5. Right-click the second key on the Z position curve to open its Key Info dialog box, click and hold the In Tangent flyout, point to the Linear tangent type button, then release the mouse button.

FIGURE 9

Curves for X Position and Z Position tracks

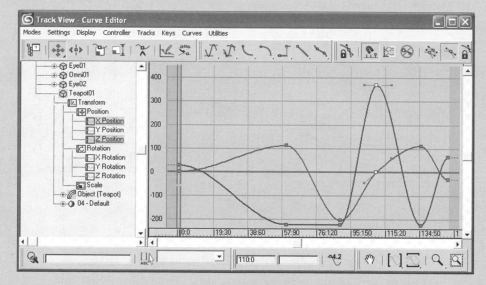

6. Click the Tangent copy button to the right of the In Tangent flyout to copy the tangent type to the Out tangent, then close the Key Info dialog box.

7. Right-click the second key on the X position curve to open its Key Info dialog box, click and hold the In Tangent flyout, point to the Linear tangent type button, release the mouse button, then click the Tangent copy button to the right of the In Tangent flyout to copy the tangent type to the Out tangent. The curves in the Curve Editor should now resemble Figure 10.

8. Close the X Position Key Info dialog box, then close the Curve Editor.

9. Switch to the Front viewport, then notice that the ticks on the trajectory for the teapot are much more evenly spaced around its second key, due to the change to Linear tangents for the X and Z position keys.

10. Switch back to the Perspective viewport, play the animation a few times, stop the animation, then save the file as **Eyes06**.

FIGURE 10

X Position key with tangent types changed

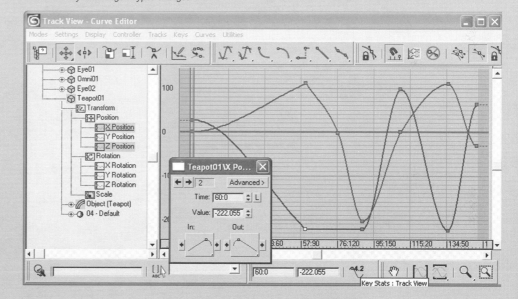

Assign animation controllers.

1. Click the Motion tab on the Command panel; open the Assign Controller rollout; click the plus sign next to the Position track in the controllers list; then select the X Position, Y Position, and Z Position tracks at the same time.

2. Click the Assign Controller button, then double-click Linear Float to assign the Linear Float controller to each of the teapot's position tracks.

3. Open the Curve Editor, then select the X, Y, and Z Position tracks in the Controller window. The curves for the position tracks should look similar to those shown in Figure 11, with linear In and Out tangents for each key.

4. Close the Curve Editor, play the animation to see the effect of the new controller on the motion of the teapot, stop the animation, then save the file as **Eyes07**.

FIGURE 11

Position track curves with Linear Float controller assigned

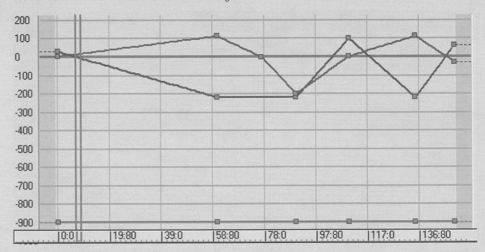

Assign animation constraints.

1. Select the eyeball on the left, click the Motion tab, click the Rotation track in the Assign Controllers list, click the Assign Controller button, then double-click the LookAt Constraint in the Assign Rotation Controller dialog box.

2. Click the Add LookAt Target button in the LookAt Constraint rollout on the Motion panel, then click the teapot in the scene.

3. Click the Add LookAt Target button to deselect it, then click the Z option button in the Select LookAt Axis group in the LookAt Constraint rollout so that the iris and pupil of the eyeball are aimed at the teapot.

4. Select the eyeball on the right, click the Motion tab, click the Rotation track in the Assign Controllers list, click the Assign Controller button, then double-click the LookAt Constraint in the Assign Rotation Controller dialog box.

5. Click the Add LookAt Target button in the LookAt Constraint rollout on the Motion panel, click the teapot, click the Add LookAt Target button to deselect it, then click the Z option button in the Select LookAt Axis group in the LookAt Constraint rollout.

6. Play the animation. The eyes should follow the teapot as it moves during the animation.

7. Stop the animation, move the time slider to frame 100, then render the scene. Your scene should look similar to Figure 12.

8. Save the file as **Eyes08**, then reset 3ds Max.

FIGURE 12
Scene rendered at frame 100

PROJECT BUILDER 1

You are at your first job at a video game company and have been asked to animate some objects in order to test how they look as they move. The first object you need to animate is a fighter jet, which you need to animate to look as though it is banking during flight.

1. Open MAXWB06-02.max from the drive and directory where your Data Files are stored.
2. Create a free camera in the scene, create a Camera viewport, then turn on Safe Frames in the viewport.
3. Adjust the viewport until it shows the plane at an angle, fairly close up, with room between the plane and the action safe frame.
4. With the time slider at frame 0, switch to the Top viewport and move the plane until it is slightly offscreen to the left in the Camera viewport.
5. Turn on Auto Key, move the time slider to the last frame in the animation, move the plane so that it is slightly offscreen to the right in the Camera viewport, then turn off Auto Key.
6. Move the time slider until the plane is partly onscreen in the Camera viewport, click the Key Filters button, deselect all but the Rotation check box, close the Set Key Filters dialog box, then click the Toggle Set Key Mode button to turn Set Key on.
7. Click the Set Keys button to set a rotation key, move the time slider so that the plane is entirely within the title safe frame, rotate it about 45 degrees around its y-axis so that it banks toward the camera, then click the Set Keys button.
8. Move the time slider again until the nose of the plane is out of the action safe frame, rotate the plane 90 degrees so that it banks away from the camera, then click the Set Keys button.

9. Move the time slider so that the plane is just out of the title safe frame, rotate it 45 degrees around its y-axis so that it is righted (not banking), click the Set Keys button, then turn off Set Key mode.

10. Play the animation. The plane should bank toward and away from the camera, then right itself as it leaves the scene. At frame 50, your scene should look similar to Figure 13.

11. Save the file as **FighterJet**, then reset 3ds Max.

12. Copy the Top.tif file from your Data Files folder to the same folder as the FighterJet file, since the Top.tif file is used in the FighterJet scene.

FIGURE 13
Completed Project Builder 1

PROJECT BUILDER 2

As a designer at a video game company, you are working on a video game scene in which a rocket races through a tunnel. In this part of the scene, however, the tunnel is viewed from the point of view of the rocket traveling through it. To create this scene, you decide to use a camera to represent the rocket and animate the camera following a path.

1. Create a large circle spline in the Top viewport, then create a small circle spline.

2. Insert two new smooth vertices in the large circle spline, moving them out of the original circle spline to create an irregular shape.

3. Create a loft object with the small circle as the shape and the large circle as a path.

4. In the Skin Parameters rollout for the loft object, increase the number of Path Steps to **24** to add more segments to the object, then flip the normals of the object.

5. Create a free camera in the Front viewport, click the Motion tab, assign the Path Constraint to the camera's Position track, click the Add Path button, then click the large circle spline to select it as the camera's path.

6. In the Path Parameters rollout, click the Follow check box in the Path Options group to select it, then click the X, Y, or Z option button in the Axis group so that the camera

is aimed in the direction it travels along the path.

7. Change the Perspective viewport into a Camera viewport, then play the animation.

8. Assign the Checker map to the Diffuse component of a material in the Material Editor; change the number in the U Tiling box of the map's coordinates rollout to **15** and the number in the V Tiling box to **32**; change Color #1 and Color #2 to bright, contrasting

colors; then apply the material to the loft object.

9. Re-scale the animation so that its End Time is **200** and the camera moves more slowly through the tunnel.

10. Insert an omni light in the scene, instance the light several times, then place the lights at an even distance apart within the loft object, as shown in Figure 14.

FIGURE 14
Lights placed within loft object

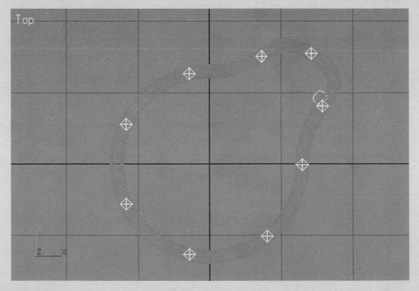

11. Activate the Camera viewport, then play the animation. The camera view during the animation should look similar to Figure 15.

12. Save the file as **Camera Tunnel**, then reset 3ds Max.

FIGURE 15
Completed Project Builder 2

PROJECT BUILDER 3

As a student of animation, sometimes you can learn a lot about animation simply by trying to duplicate a simple motion encountered in the real world. Animating simple motions can actually take a great deal of time, because you need to carefully create the timing and parameter changes that will reproduce the motion accurately. Even as you gain more experience as an animator, you'll find that working through basic exercises – such as creating a bouncing ball, which you'll do in this Project Builder – enables you to improve your skills even further.

1. Create a sphere, click the Base to Pivot check box in its Parameters rollout, then maximize the Left viewport and adjust it so that the sphere is in the bottom left of the viewport.

2. Turn on Auto Key, move the time slider to frame 15, then move the ball up and to the right to create the first half of its first bounce.

3. Copy the key from frame 0 to frame 30, then select and move the sphere to the right along its x-axis so that it is in the correct location for coming down at the end of its first bounce.

4. Turn on the trajectory for the sphere, then adjust the keyframe at the top of the bounce as necessary so that the bounce trajectory is symmetrical and looks like a more realistic bounce when the animation is played.

5. Create a second, lower bounce for the ball by creating keys at frames 45 and 60, adjusting the frame 45 key as necessary to create a more realistic bounce.

6. Turn off Auto Key, then play the animation.

7. Select all of the sphere's keys and move them so that the start of the first bounce is at frame 30, then animate the sphere dropping from a location at frame 0 to the location at frame 30 where its first bounce starts. Keep in mind that it should be dropped from a location higher than the peak of the first bounce.

8. Increase the active time segment length to **150**, then insert keys at frames 75, 90, 105, and 120 to animate the sphere bouncing twice more, lower each time.

9. Decrease the time between bounces after the first bounce to reflect the fact that the bounces will be shorter as the ball bounces lower.

10. Animate the sphere to roll away from the end of its last bounce for about one second.

11. Open the Curve Editor, select the curve for the sphere's Y Position tracks, delete all but its start and end keyframes, then change the Out tangent of its first key to a linear tangent type and copy the linear tangent type to the In tangent of its last key.

12. Select the X Position track, delete all of its keyframes, then select the Z Position track.

13. Since the speed of a bouncing ball increases as it falls and slows as it approaches the peak of a bounce, change the In and Out tangents of the first key and the keys at the peaks of the bounces to Slow tangent types, then change the In and Out tangents of the keys at the bounces to Fast tangent types. When the tangent types have been changed, the ball's trajectory should look like Figure 16.

14. Play the animation, then adjust the keyframes further as necessary to make the bounces as realistic as possible.

FIGURE 16
Trajectory after tangent types modified

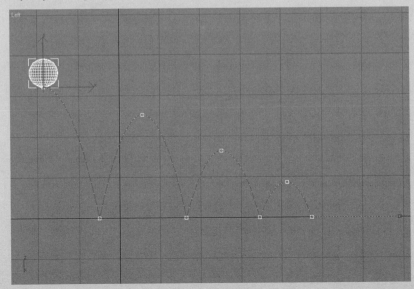

15. Select the sphere at frame 0, apply the Stretch modifier to it, then animate the Stretch value of the modifier so that the ball is squashed when it bounces and at the peaks of the bounces, and stretched between the bounces and bounce peaks.

16. Open the Dope Sheet; open the Sphere01 heading in the Controller window; open the Modified Object heading; open the Stretch heading; then select the Stretch track under the Stretch heading. Adjust the keys for the Stretch track to ensure that the stretching amount of the ball is at its peak just before it hits the ground and is squashed. Figure 17 shows what the keys for the Stretch value animation track might look like.

17. Create a large plane under the ball and apply a dark green material to it, then apply a shiny red material to the ball.

18. Add an omni light to the scene high above the ball, then turn its shadows on.

19. Insert a camera in the scene, create a Camera viewport, turn on Safe Frames, then adjust the camera view so that the ball falls into the action safe frame of the view, bounces within it, then rolls and stops on its far right.

FIGURE 17

Curve for the Stretch value animation track

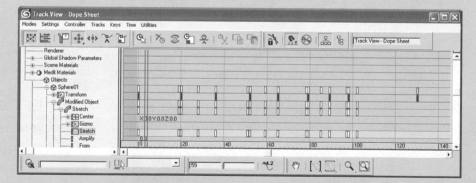

20. Play the animation in the camera viewport, and make any adjustments necessary to increase the realism. Figure 18 shows what the scene should look like just before the third bounce.

21. Save the file as **BouncingBall**, then reset 3ds Max.

FIGURE 18

Completed Project Builder 3

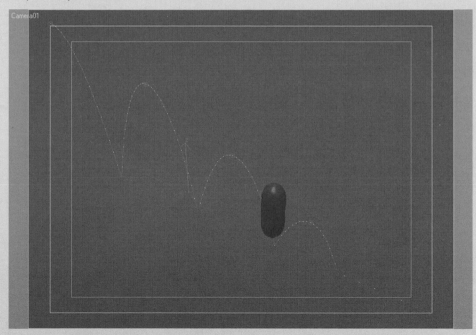

DESIGN PROJECT

You are one of a group of freelance animators creating animations to be used by an advertising agency in a commercial for a chain of family entertainment centers. One animator is animating billiards being played on a pool table, one is animating a ball being putted into a miniature golf hole, and you are in charge of creating a dart hitting the bullseye of a dartboard. Because you haven't played darts much, you do a little research before creating the animation.

1. Use online or other resources to locate a picture of a dart and a dartboard.
2. Use the Lathe modifier to create the shape of the body of the dart, then use other modeling techniques to create the tail of the dart.
3. Apply a variety of materials to the dart to give it a realistic look.
4. Model a dartboard, position it as though it is hanging on a wall, then apply materials to it to give it a realistic look.
5. Set up a camera in the scene, aim the camera at the dartboard, then create a Camera viewport using Safe Frames.
6. Animate the dart flying in and hitting the center of the dartboard. The dart should be entirely within the camera viewport before it hits the dartboard in the animation.

7. Animate the position of the camera so that it zooms in on the dartboard before the dart hits it, then zooms out from the dartboard after the dart hits it.
8. Add lighting and shadows to the scene so that the dartboard is lit, and so that the area through which the dart travels is lit as well. Figure 19 shows an example of what a final scene might look like.
9. Save the file as **Dart**, then reset 3ds Max.

FIGURE 19

Example of completed Design Project

PORTFOLIO PROJECT

You've been hired by a Web site that sells stock animation footage to create an animation of a marble traveling through a maze. Once you create the animation and render it, the site will then make the animation available to be purchased and downloaded by anyone who needs the animation for something, such as for the background of a presentation. You decide to create the maze using an extruded spline and consider a number of ways to animate the marble traveling through the maze.

1. Create a maze for the marble to travel through by creating an editable spline or splines, using snap to make the paths within the maze even in size. Next, extrude the spline(s) to create a maze with walls. Feel free to use Figure 20 as a model to base your maze on.

2. Insert a large plane in the scene for the maze to rest on.

3. Create and apply materials to the maze and the plane so that the plane is a light color and the maze is darker by contrast.

4. Insert a sphere into the scene appropriately sized to fit in the maze, then create and apply the material necessary to make the sphere look like a marble.

5. Create bright lighting in the scene. Use a skylight if possible.

6. Determine how you will animate the marble through the maze. You might use a Path constraint on the sphere so that it follows a path through the maze, or you might animate its position using Auto Key to have it travel through the maze.

7. Animate the marble through the maze, adjusting the timing and active time segment of the animation as necessary as you work.

8. Set up a camera in the scene aimed at the maze at an attractive angle, then create a Camera viewport for the camera using Safe Frames.

9. Render the Camera viewport at the animation's halfway point. An example of what the scene might look like is shown in Figure 21.

10. Save the file as **Maze**, then reset 3ds Max.

FIGURE 20
Example maze created with editable spline

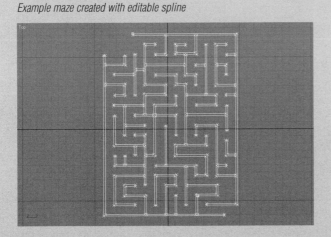

FIGURE 21
Example of completed Portfolio Project

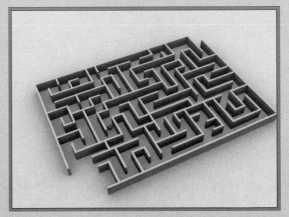

chapter

7 RENDERING

1. What is rendering?

2. Render with ActiveShade.

3. Understand file output.

4. Create and save renderings.

5. Use the Print Size Wizard.

CHAPTER SUMMARY

In this chapter, you learned what rendering is, what renderers are, and which renderers are available with 3ds Max. You also learned about ActiveShade rendering and used it to preview scenes in detail without going through a full rendering process. You learned about the file formats that can be produced with rendering, and explored their different uses. You learned about video codecs and resolution considerations and how each can be a factor as you plan how to render a scene to a file. You used the Common panel in the Render Scene dialog box, adjusted the settings on the Common panel to get the desired file output, and rendered files from the dialog box. Lastly, you used the Print Size Wizard to render scenes with the settings necessary to create files appropriate for print media.

FIGURE 1
Rendering a scene

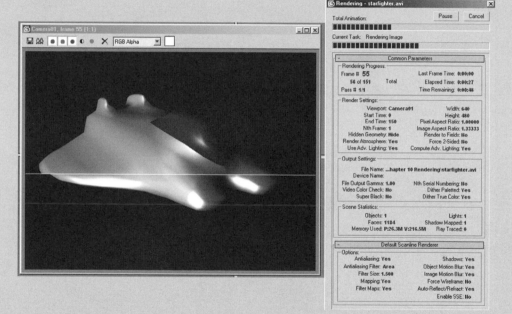

SKILLS REFERENCE

to do this:	use this method:
Activate the ActiveShade window as a floater	
Adjust the amount of compression to apply with a codec	Adjust the Quality slider in the compression settings dialog box
Adjust the aspect ratio for an output type	Choose Custom as the Output Size type, then adjust the number in the Image Aspect field in the Output Size group
Change the number that appears at the end of the first file in an image file sequence	Change the number in the File Number Base box in the Time Output box in the Render Scene dialog box
Change the renderer to the default scanline renderer	Click Rendering on the menu bar, click Render, open the Assign Renderer rollout at the bottom of the Common panel, click the Choose Renderer button to the right of Production or ActiveShade, click Default Scanline Renderer, then click OK
Change the renderer to the mental ray renderer	Click Rendering on the menu bar, click Render, open the Assign Renderer rollout at the bottom of the Common panel, click the Choose Renderer button to the right of Production or ActiveShade, click mental ray Renderer, then click OK

to do this:	use this method:
Change to Production or ActiveShade rendering mode	Click the Production option button or ActiveShade option button at the bottom of the Common panel in the Render Scene dialog box
Choose a DPI setting in the Print Size Wizard	Click the 72, 150, 300, or 600 button in the Paper Size group **or** Enter an exact dots-per-inch setting in the DPI box in the Paper Size group
Choose a paper size in the Print Size Wizard	Click the Paper Size list arrow, then click a preset paper size **or** Click the Paper Size list arrow, click Custom (if necessary), then enter the paper size settings in the Paper Width and Paper Height boxes or the Image Width and Image Height boxes
Choose a resolution for an output type	Click a resolution button in the Output Size group in the Render Scene dialog box **or** Enter a pixel dimension in the Width or Height fields in the Output Size group in the Render Scene dialog box
Choose a video codec	Click the Compressor list arrow in the compression settings dialog box, then click the name of the codec

to do this:	use this method:
Determine output resolution for a printed image	Width pixels × height pixels = (DPI × width inches) × (DPI × height inches)
Dock the ActiveShade window in place of a viewport	Right-click the viewport label, point to Views, then click ActiveShade
Draw a region in an ActiveShade window to be updated	Right-click in the ActiveShade window, click Draw Region, then click and drag in the window to create a region
Initialize an ActiveShade window	Right-click in the ActiveShade window, then click Initialize
Open the Print Size Wizard	Click Rendering on the menu bar, then click Print Size Wizard
Open the Render Scene dialog box	 **or** Click Rendering on the menu bar, then click Render **or** Press [F10]

to do this:	use this method:
Render a range of frames in an active time segment	Click the Range option button in the Time Output group in the Render Scene dialog box, then enter the start frame and end frame in the Range fields
Render a scene	 **or** Click the Render button in the Render Scene dialog box
Render a scene as a certain file type	Click the Files button in the Render Output group in the Render Scene dialog box, navigate to a location to save the rendered file(s), name the file(s), click the Save as type list arrow, click a file type, then click Save
Render a scene from the Print Size Wizard	Click the Quick Render button in the Print Size Wizard **or** Click the Render Scene Dialog button in the Print Size Wizard, adjust any settings desired in the Render Scene dialog box, then click the Render button in the Render Scene dialog box
Render a TIFF file from the Print Size Wizard	Click the Files button, select a location for the TIFF file, click Save, then click the Quick Render button

to do this:	use this method:
Render an image file sequence	Render a range of frames from an animation in a still picture format
Render frames in an animation at intervals	Click the Active Time Segment option button in the Time Output group in the Render Scene dialog box, then enter a number in the Every Nth Frame box to set the interval
Render specific frames	Click the Frames option button in the Time Output group in the Render Scene dialog box, the enter the frame numbers in the Frames field
Render the active time segment	Click the Active Time Segment option button in the Time Output group in the Render Scene dialog box
Render the current frame	Click the Single option button in the Time Output group in the Render Scene dialog box
Select a preset output size type	Click the Output Size list arrow in the Render Scene dialog box, then click a preset output

Render with ActiveShade.

1. Open MAXWB07-01.max from the drive and directory containing your Data Files.
2. Click and hold the Quick Render (Production) tool, then click the Quick Render (ActiveShade) tool to open the ActiveShade window as a floater.
3. Open the Material Editor, select the Walls material in the upper left slot, then change the Diffuse component color to bright red.
4. Right-click the ActiveShade window, then click Initialize.
5. After the ActiveShade window has reinitialized, right-click the ActiveShade window again, click Draw Region on the right-click menu, then draw a region around the upper right area of the glass.
6. Change the Diffuse component color for the Walls material to light green, right-click the ActiveShade window, then click Initialize. The window should update within the region, as shown in Figure 2.
7. Save the file as **RenderedGlass**, then close the ActiveShade window.

FIGURE 2

Updated region in ActiveShade window

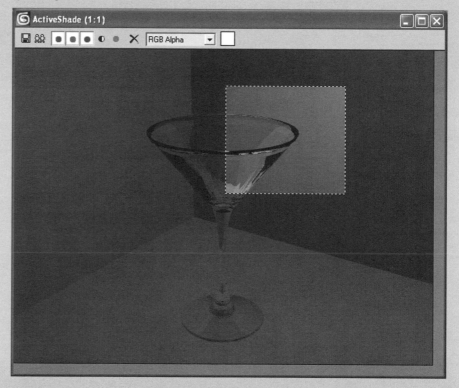

Create and save renderings.

1. Click in the Perspective viewport, click Views on the menu bar, then click Create Camera from View.
2. Right-click the Camera viewport label, then click Show Safe Frame.
3. Click the Toggle Auto Key Mode button, move the time slider to frame 100, then dolly the camera forward in the Camera viewport so that the view zooms in slightly on the glass.
4. Turn Auto Key off, then play the animation a few times.
5. Click the Render Scene Dialog tool, click the Production option button at the bottom of the dialog box, click the Active Time Segment option button in the Time Output group, enter **10** in the Every Nth Frame box, then click the 720 × 486 button in the Output Size group.
6. Click the Files button in the Render Output group, navigate to your Data Files drive and directory, name the file **Glass**, click the Save as type list arrow, click AVI File (*.avi), then click Save.
7. Click OK in the AVI File Compression Setup dialog box, then click Render in the Render Scene dialog box.
8. When the scene has finished rendering, click the Render Scene Dialog tool, click the Range option button in the Time Output group, enter **10** as the start frame and **15** as the end frame of the range, then change the number in the Every Nth Frame box to **1**.
9. Click the Files button in the Render Output group, create and open a folder within your Data Files directory named **Sequence**, click the Save as type list arrow, click JPEG file (*.jpg, *.jpe, *.jpeg), click Save, click OK, then click the Render button.
10. Open the Glass.avi file from your Data Files directory, then play the animation.
11. Move the slider in the media player to about the halfway point in the animation. The AVI file should look similar to Figure 3.

FIGURE 3
Glass AVI file

12. Close the media player window, then open the Sequence folder in your Data Files directory. Its contents should look like Figure 4.
13. Return to 3ds Max, then save the scene as **RenderedGlass01**.

FIGURE 4

Contents of Sequence folder

Name	Size	Type	Date Modi...	▼	Dimensions
Glass0010	12 KB	Paint S...	11/29/200...		720 x 486
Glass0011	12 KB	Paint S...	11/29/200...		720 x 486
Glass0012	12 KB	Paint S...	11/29/200...		720 x 486
Glass0013	12 KB	Paint S...	11/29/200...		720 x 486
Glass0014	12 KB	Paint S...	11/29/200...		720 x 486
Glass0015	12 KB	Paint S...	11/29/200...		720 x 486

Use the Print Size Wizard.

1. Click Rendering on the menu bar, then click Print Size Wizard.
2. Click the Paper Size list arrow, then click B – 17 × 11in.
3. Click the 150 DPI button, then click the Portrait option button.
4. Click the Files button in the Rendering group, navigate to the drive and directory where you save your files (if necessary), name the file **Glass**, click Save, then click the Quick Render button in the Print Size window.
5. Open the Glass.tif file using an appropriate graphics program. The file should look similar to Figure 5.
6. Close the rendered scene window, save the file as **RenderedGlass02**, then reset 3ds Max.

FIGURE 5

Glass.tif file

PROJECT BUILDER 1

As an industrial designer working for a light manufacturer, you have come up with a new type of chandelier for this year's line and created a lit scene containing a model of the light. The image you have created of the light will be included in a full-color brochure describing the forthcoming designs, and it will also be used on the manufacturer's Web site. You've been asked to render the image as a file that can be used in print and as a separate file that can be used on the Web.

1. Open the file MAXWB07-02.max or the Chandelier.max file you created in Chapter 5, then open the Print Size Wizard.

2. Select 11 × 8.5 inches as the Paper Size, then click the 300 DPI button.

3. Click the Files button in the Rendering group, navigate to your Data Files drive and directory, name the file **Chandelier**, click Save, then click the Quick Render button to render the scene as a TIFF file. It may take a while for the file to render because of the high DPI setting.

4. Close the rendered scene, then click the Render Scene Dialog button in the Print Size Wizard.

5. Click the Files button in the Render Output group, navigate to your Data Files drive and directory, name the file **Chandelier**, choose the JPEG file type, click Save, then click OK in the JPEG Image Control dialog box.

6. Click the Render button in the Render Scene dialog box.

7. Open Chandelier.tif and Chandelier.jpg, as shown in Figure 6. On-screen, the TIFF file should have a higher quality appearance than the JPEG file.

8. Close the files, then reset 3ds Max.

FIGURE 6

Completed Project Builder 1

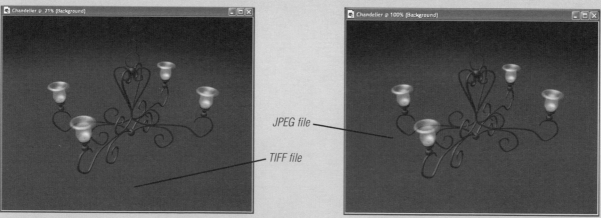

JPEG file

TIFF file

PROJECT BUILDER 2

You are a freelance animator who has created an animation of a dart hitting the bullseye of a dartboard for a client to use on television. They have asked you to render two separate files of the animation, in two different formats—one that they can use in a television commercial and one that will appear as a movie on the Web.

1. Open MAXWB07-03.max or the Dart.max file you created in Chapter 6.

2. Open the Render Scene dialog box, click the Active Time Segment option button, then set the Output Size resolution to 720 × 486.

3. Click the Files button, navigate to your Data Files drive and directory, name the file **DartboardTV**, choose the AVI file type, click Save, click OK in the AVI File Compression Setup dialog box, then render the file.

4. Close the rendered scene window, then change the Output Size resolution to 320 × 240.

5. Click the Files button, name the file **DartboardWeb**, choose the MOV QuickTime File (*.mov) file type, then click Save.

6. Click the list arrow at the top of the Compression Settings dialog box, click Sorenson Video to select the Sorenson

video codec, move the Quality slider all the way to the right to Best, click OK, then render the animation. Notice that the MOV file, which will be used on the Web, takes less time to render than the AVI file due to its smaller resolution.

7. Open DartboardTV.avi and play the animation, then open DartboardWeb.mov and play the animation. Figure 7 shows what each file might look like in a media player.

8. Close the media player, close the rendered scene window, then reset 3ds Max.

FIGURE 7

Completed Project Builder 2

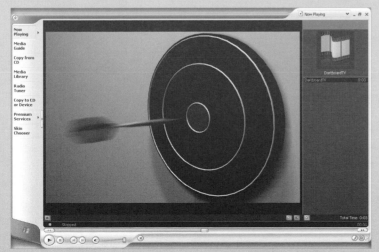

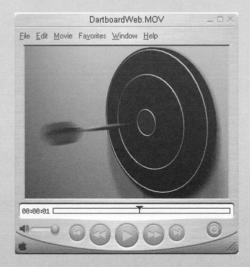

PROJECT BUILDER 3

You work for an architect creating digital images of planned projects. You have created a visual of a planned room lit by a table lamp on top of a table, and inserted a camera into the scene to control from which point the room is viewed. The architect wants to include an animation showing the room from the point of view of the camera as it rotates 360 degrees in the center of the room. Because the room only contains the table and the lamp, you add some more items to the room that will help orient the viewer as he or she views the animation. The animation will be included in a professional video, and the video editor needs to be able to work with each individual image, although you're not sure what kind of video editing software the editor will use. You determine that creating an image file sequence of the animation using the TIFF file format will enable the video editor to use any number of different software options to edit the images.

1. Open MAXWB07-04.max or the LampRoom.max file you created in Chapter 5.
2. Change the camera into a free camera, then position it in the scene in the center of the room.
3. Add some objects around the room so that at least one object is next to or on each wall in the room.
4. Animate the camera so that it does a 360-degree turn in place around the room in 3 seconds.
5. Play the animation, make any changes needed to the scene before rendering, then save the scene as **360 Degrees**.
6. Render the active time segment as an image file sequence of TIFF files named **CameraView** in a folder called **RoomSequence**. The resolution for the files should be 720 × 486.

7. When rendering is completed, change the settings in the Render Scene dialog box so that only the current frame will be rendered on-screen and not saved to a file; move the time slider to frame 70; then render the frame.

8. Open the RoomSequence folder, then open CameraView0070.tif. CameraView0070.tif should look the same as frame 70 in the animation, as shown in Figure 8.

9. Close CameraView0070.tif, close the rendered scene window in 3ds Max, then reset 3ds Max.

FIGURE 8

Example of completed Project Builder 3

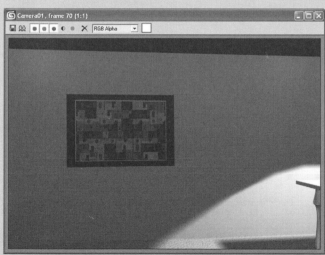
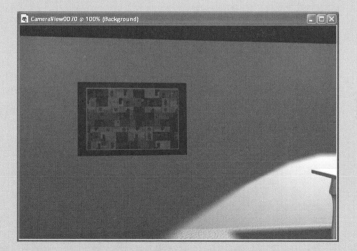

DESIGN PROJECT

You work in design at a marketing company and have created an image of a chess piece to be used on a postcard to be sent to potential attendees of a business strategy seminar. Now that the image is completed, you need to render the file into a format that the printer can use to print the postcard, and as a file that can be used on the Web site containing the seminar information. The postcard will be 5 × 7 inches in size, but you'll render the file as an image larger than the card size. This is so that the designer putting the card together has some leeway with how the image appears on the card and can shift or crop it as needed. Another reason to make the image larger is to account for the small variations in where the postcards are cut at the printer, so that white space around the image doesn't accidentally show up on any of the cards.

1. Open MAXWB07-05 or the Strategy.max file you created in Chapter 5.
2. Open the Print Size Wizard, then select a paper size of 11 × 8.5.
3. Click the Files button, then save the file as **StrategyCard** in your Data Files drive and directory.
4. Render the file, then open the Render Scene dialog box from the Print Size Wizard.
5. Change the resolution to 320 × 240, save the file as **StrategyWeb.jpg** in your Data Files drive and directory, then render the scene.
6. Open StrategyCard.tif and StrategyWeb.jpg, as shown in Figure 9.
7. Close StrategyCard.tif and StrategyWeb.jpg, then reset 3ds Max.

FIGURE 9
Example of completed Design Project

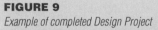

In your first job at a video game company, you previously created a fighter jet and animated it to show how it looked as it moved. You now have been asked to create a separate animation of the jet in which it flies in front of a moving background, and to render the file so that you can check how the animation looks when played in a media player.

1. Open the Material Editor, then, using a file found in the 3dsMax8/maps/ folder or that you find online, assign a bitmap that depicts an outdoor background (such as sky, a satellite photo of the ground, buildings, or a landscape) to the Diffuse component of a material.

2. In the Top viewport, create a large plane, then apply the mapped material to the plane.

3. Zoom in on the plane in the viewport until its outer edges are outside the viewport boundaries; adjust the view so that the left side of the plane is in the center of the viewport; turn on Auto Key; then animate the movement of the plane from right to left between frames 0 and 100, without showing its edges in the viewport.

4. Turn on Smooth + Highlights in the viewport, then play the animation. The image should move slowly from right to left.

5. Render the active time segment of the scene as an AVI file named **JetBackground**.

6. When rendering is complete, save the file as **JetBackground.max**, then open MAXWB07-06.max.

7. Click Rendering on the menu bar, click Environment, click the Environment Map map button, navigate to the JetBackground.avi file you just created, then double-click it.

8. Click Views on the menu bar, click Viewport Background, click the Use Environment Background check box in the Viewport Background dialog box to select it, click OK, then render the Perspective viewport to see the background behind the jet.

9. Animate the fighter jet in the file so that it appears to be flying in front of the background, banking a couple of times and changing direction. Depending on the background you use, you might animate it flying low to the ground in front of a landscape background, or show it from the top as it flies over the ground far below.

10. Turn on the jet's trajectory, then add a directional light to the scene whose hotspot and falloff encompass the entire trajectory so that the jet will be lit throughout the animation.

11. Render the active time segment of the scene to an AVI file called **JetFly**, using a resolution of 720×486.

12. When rendering is complete, play the JetFly.avi file. Figure 10 shows an example of what the animation might look like at two points, one early in the animation and one just before it ends. The background in the animation should move as it is played.

13. Close your media player, save the scene as **JetFly.max**, then reset 3ds Max.

FIGURE 10

Example of completed Portfolio Project

chapter

8 BONES AND
INVERSE KINEMATICS

1. Create bones.

2. Create bones within a character mesh.

3. Edit bones.

4. Apply inverse kinematics.

5. Use skin.

6. Animate bones.

CHAPTER SUMMARY

In this chapter, you learned what bones are and how they are used within a character. You created a chain of bones, named the bones, and manipulated bones by working with their pivot points. You made a character mesh see-through and froze the mesh to more easily work with bones. You used the Bone Tools floater to build a bone structure. You adjusted the size and taper of bones in a character rig, added fins to the bones, and adjusted the size and taper settings of the fins. You gained an understanding of inverse kinematics and used it to affect the normal behavior of a bone hierarchy. You used dummy objects to control bones when animating them, and used skinning to have bones and character mesh move together. Finally, you created an animation of the bones within a character and looped the animation to produce a continuous motion of the bones.

FIGURE 1

Character with head, neck, body, and tail bones

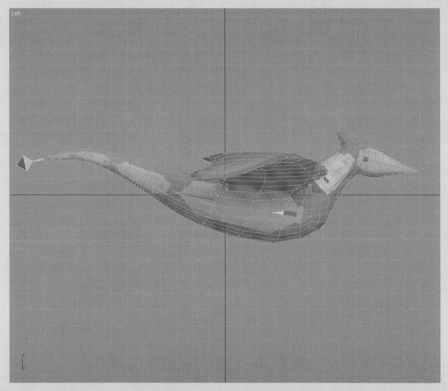

SKILLS REFERENCE

to do this:	use this method:
Add fins to a bone or bones	Select the bone, click the Modify tab, then click the Side Fins, Front Fin, and/or Back Fin check box in the Bone Fins group in the Bone Parameters rollout **or** Select the bone or bones; open the Fin Adjustment Tools rollout on the Bone Tools floater; then click the Side Fins, Front Fin, and/or Back Fin check box
Adjust a fin's size and/or taper settings	Adjust the Size, Start Taper, and/or End Taper settings in the Bone Fins group in the Bone Parameters rollout on the Modify panel **or** Adjust the Size, Start Taper, and/or End Taper settings in the Fin Adjustment Tools rollout on the Bone Tools floater
Adjust how much a bone tapers along its length	Adjust the Taper setting in the Bone Objects group in the Fin Adjustment Tools rollout on the Bone Tools floater **or** Adjust the Taper setting in the Bone Object group in the Bone Parameters rollout on the Modify panel
Adjust the length of a bone	Enter Bone Edit Mode, then reposition the bone's pivot point **or** Enter Bone Edit Mode, then reposition the pivot point of the bone's child bone
Adjust the size of a bone's envelope	Select and move a handle on one of the envelope's cross sections

to do this:	use this method:
Adjust the width and/or height of a bone	Adjust the Width and/or Height settings in the Bone Objects group in the Fin Adjustment Tools rollout on the Bone Tools floater **or** Adjust the Width and/or Height settings in the Bone Object group in the Bone Parameters rollout on the Modify panel
Apply the HI Solver to a bone chain	Select the bone where you want the IK chain to begin, click Animation on the menu bar, point to IK Solvers, click HI Solver, then click the bone where you want the IK chain to end **or** Click the end effector bone, click Animation on the menu bar, point to IK Solvers, click HI Solver, and then click the bone where you want the IK chain to begin
Apply the SplineIK Solver to a bone chain	Select the first bone in the chain, click Animation on the menu bar, point to IK Solvers, click SplineIK Solver, click the last bone in the bone chain, then click the spline to which you want the bones to conform
Change the weight of a vertex within a bone's envelope	Enter Edit Envelopes mode, then adjust the size of the inner or outer envelope **or** In Edit Envelopes mode, click the Vertices check box in the Parameters rollout, select a vertex, select the name in the Bones list of the bone for which you want to change the vertex weight, then change the Abs. Effect value in the Weight Properties group

to do this:	use this method:
Create a dummy object	Click 🔲 , click the Dummy button in the Object Type rollout, then click and drag in a viewport
Create a master control	Create a dummy object in the scene, then link all the movable components of a rig to it
Create bones	Click the Create Bones button, click in a viewport, click again in the viewport to create the first bone, continue clicking to create the bones needed, then right-click to end bone creation **or** Click ⚞ , click the Bones button in the Object Type rollout, click in a viewport, click again in the viewport to create the first bone, continue clicking to create the bones needed, then right-click to end bone creation
Delete a chain of bones	Double-click the root parent bone to select the chain, then press [Delete]
Delete a nub bone	Select the nub, then press [Delete]
Enter Edit Envelopes mode	Select mesh to which the Skin modifier has been applied, click the Modify tab, select the Skin modifier in the modifier stack, and then click the Edit Envelopes button in the Parameters rollout
Enter or exit bone creation mode	Click the Bones button in the Object Type rollout on the Systems panel **or** Click the Create Bones button on the Bone Tools floater

to do this:	use this method:
Enter or exit Bone Edit Mode	Click the Bone Edit Mode button at the top of the Bone Tools floater
Freeze an object	Select the object, right-click in any viewport, then select Freeze Selection on the Display quadrant of the Quad menu
Link an object to a dummy object	
Loop an animation	Select the object whose action you want to loop, open Track View, click , click the Loop graph in the Param Curves Out-of-Range dialog box, then click OK
Make an object see-through	Right-click the object, click Properties on the Transform quadrant of the Quad menu, select the See-Through check box, then click OK **or** Select the object, then press [Alt][x]
Open the Bone Tools floater	Click Character on the menu bar, then click Bone Tools
Rename a bone	Select the bone, double-click the default name in the text box at the top of the Modify panel, then type a new name

to do this:	use this method:
Reposition a bone's pivot point	Enter Bone Edit Mode, then drag the bone's pivot point in the direction you want to move it
Rotate a bone around its own pivot point	Click ↻ , then rotate the bone
Rotate a bone around its parent's pivot point	Click ✛ , then move the bone
Skin a mesh	Apply the Skin modifier to a mesh, click the Add button next to Bones in the modifier's Parameters rollout on the Modify panel, select the bones in the mesh in the Select Bones dialog box, then click Select
Test skin deformation	Animate the movement of bones within a mesh from a stationary position, scrub the time slider back and forth to view the deformation, adjust the size and position of the envelopes in the stationary keyframe to fix issues, adjust vertex weights manually if necessary, then test again
Unfreeze an object	Right-click in any viewport, then select Unfreeze All on the Display quadrant of the Quad menu

Create bones.

1. Create a cylinder in the Top viewport with a radius of 25, height of 250, and 15 height segments.

2. Click the Systems button on the Create panel, click the Bones button in the Object Type rollout, click at the bottom right of the cylinder in the Front viewport, move the mouse up and to the left, click again, move the mouse up, click again, move the mouse up and to the top right of the cylinder, click again, then right-click to end bone creation. The cylinder and bone chain should look similar to Figure 2.

3. Select and move the bottom bone (Bone01) until it is entirely to the right of the cylinder.

4. Select and rotate Bone02 around its y-axis by 90 degrees, then select and move the top bone (Bone03) down as far as it will go, as shown in Figure 3.

5. Save the file as **CylinderBones**, then undo the bone moves and rotations until the bone chain is back in place within the cylinder.

FIGURE 2
Completed bone chain

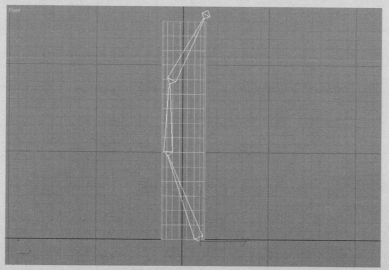

FIGURE 3
Moved and rotated bones

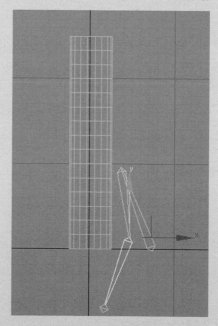

Create bones within a character mesh.

1. Press [F3] to change the shading of the Front viewport to Smooth + Highlights.
2. Select the cylinder, right-click it, then click Properties on the Transform quadrant of the Quad menu to open the Object Properties dialog box.
3. In the Display Properties group in the dialog box, click the See-Through check box to select it, then click OK.
4. Right-click in any viewport to display the Quad menu, then click Freeze Selection in the Display quadrant of the Quad menu.
5. Select Bone01. Select the text in the box at the top of the Modify panel, type **BoneBottom**, select Bone02, select the text in the box at the top of the Modify panel. Type **BoneMiddle** and then select and rename Bone03 and Bone04 as **BoneTop** and **BoneNub**, respectively.
6. Save the file as **CylinderBones01**, then compare your scene to Figure 4.

FIGURE 4
See-through and frozen cylinder

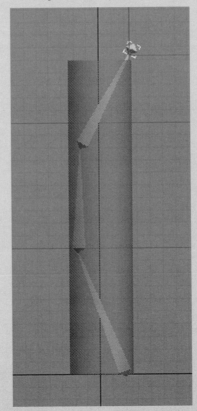

Bones and Inverse Kinematics

Edit bones.

1. Click Character on the menu bar, then click Bone Tools to open the Bone Tools floater.

2. Select BoneBottom, click the Side Fins check box in the Fin Adjustment Tools roll-out on the Bone Tools floater, change its Size value to **24.4**, click the Front Fin check box, change its Size value to **15.4**, click the Back Fin check box, then change its Size value to **17.5**.

3. Add side, front, and back fins to BoneMiddle and BoneTop with the same Size values (**24.4** for side fins, **15.4** for front fins, and **17.5** for back fins).

4. Click the Bone Edit Mode button in the Bone Tools floater, move BoneNub so that BoneTop's tip is even with the upper right edge of the cylinder in the Front viewport, move BoneTop's pivot point down so that BoneMiddle's length is shortened, then move BoneBottom's pivot point so that it is closer to the bottom center of the cylinder.

5. Click the Bone Edit Mode button to deselect it, save the file as **CylinderBones02**, then compare your scene to Figure 5.

FIGURE 5
Edited bones with fins added

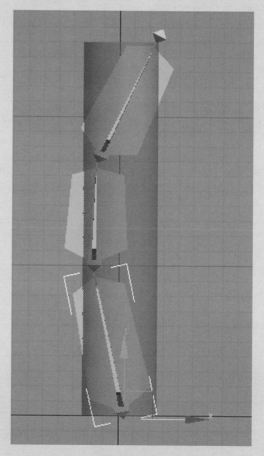

Apply inverse kinematics.

1. Select BoneBottom, click Animation on the menu bar, point to IK Solvers, click HI Solver, then click BoneNub in the viewport.

2. Save the scene as **CylinderBones03**, then compare your bones and cylinder to Figure 6.

Use skin.

1. Right-click in the viewport, click Unfreeze All on the Display quadrant of the Quad menu, then select the cylinder.

2. Click the Modify tab, click the Modifier List list arrow, then click Skin.

3. In the Parameters rollout for the Skin modifier on the Modify panel, click the Add button, highlight all of the bone objects in the list, then click Select.

4. Turn on Auto Key, move the time slider to frame 40, select the goal display, then move it down and to the right so that the cylinder is bent halfway over.

5. Move the time slider to frame 80, then move the goal display down further so that the cylinder is bent all the way over, as shown in Figure 7.

FIGURE 6
IK Solver applied to bone chain

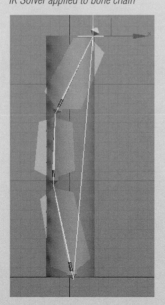

FIGURE 7
Goal display moved at frame 80

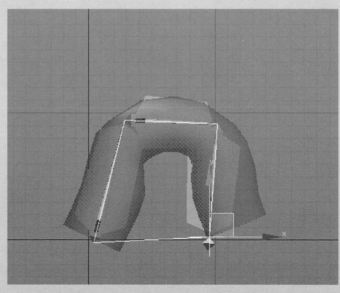

6. Turn off Auto Key, play the animation, then stop the animation and return to frame 0.

7. Select the cylinder, select the Skin modifier in the modifier stack (if necessary), click Edit Envelopes in the Parameters rollout, then select BoneTop in the Bones list in the Parameters rollout.

8. Press [F3] to display objects in wireframe in the Front viewport, increase the size of BoneTop's inner envelope until it looks like the envelope shown on the left in Figure 8, then increase BoneMiddle's inner envelope until it looks like the envelope shown on the right in Figure 8. If the inner envelopes for BoneMiddle are oriented perpendicular to the cylinder rather than parallel to it as shown in the figure, test and adjust the envelope size accordingly so that the mesh deforms as desired.

9. Save the file as **CylinderBones04**, click the Edit Envelopes button to deselect it, then play the animation again.

FIGURE 8

Edited inner envelopes for BoneTop and BoneMiddle

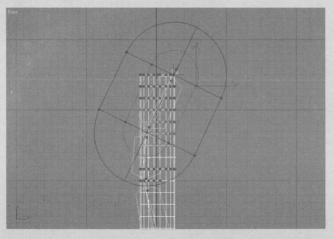 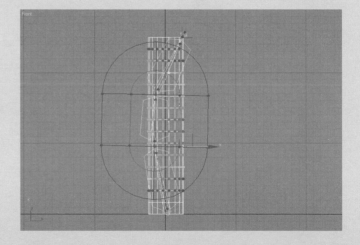

Animate bones.

1. Select the goal display, move its frame 40 and frame 80 keyframes to frame 10 and frame 50, turn on AutoKey, then move the time slider to frame 80.

2. Select BoneBottom, then move it up until the cylinder looks like Figure 9.

3. Move the time slider to frame 100, then select and move the goal display until the cylinder looks like Figure 10.

4. Turn off Auto Key, select BoneBottom, then copy its keyframe at frame 0 to frame 50.

5. Select the goal display, then copy its keyframe at frame 50 to frame 80.

6. Press [F3] to shade the objects in the scene, then play the animation.

7. Save the file as **CylinderBones05**, then reset 3ds Max.

FIGURE 9
BoneBottom moved at frame 80

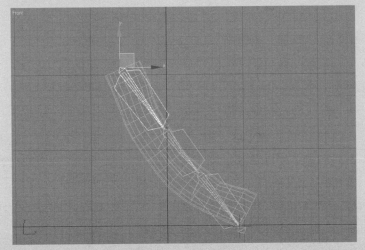

FIGURE 10
Goal display moved at frame 100

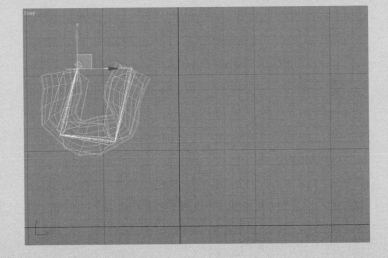

PROJECT BUILDER 1

You work for an advertising agency that is creating a commercial for a major tea company. The advertising campaign shows how the teapots in which the tea is brewed really enjoy the tea. The client has reviewed several ideas and has decided to show a teapot with a dancing spout in the commercial. Your job is to create the animation.

1. Create a teapot in the top viewport, change its Segments value to **10**, right-click in a viewport, then click Freeze Selection.
2. In the Front viewport, turn off the grid, click the Systems button on the Create panel, then click the Bones button in the Object Type rollout.
3. Create a bone chain from just inside the teapot's body through and out its spout, then create a bone and nub bone in the center of the teapot to anchor the teapot, as shown in Figure 11.
4. Unfreeze the teapot, select the teapot, then apply the Skin modifier to the teapot.
5. Click the Add button in the Parameters rollout for the modifier, select all of the bones in the Select Bones dialog box, then click Select.
6. Select each bone within the spout and move it around to see how its movement affects the teapot mesh, then undo any changes to the mesh.
7. Select the teapot, click the Edit Envelopes button in the Parameters rollout for the modifier, select each bone in the chain in the spout, then edit the envelopes as necessary so that they affect only the mesh in the spout.
8. Select the bone in the center of the teapot, then increase the size of its envelopes so that all of the mesh in the body, lid, and handle of the teapot are fully weighted, as shown in Figure 12.

FIGURE 11

Bone chains in teapot

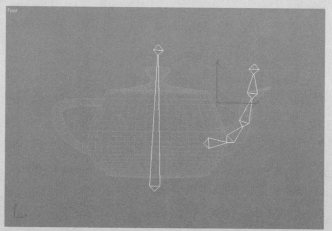

FIGURE 12

Envelopes for teapot's center bone

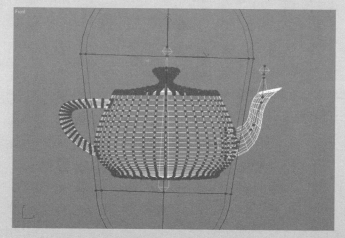

9. Exit Edit Envelopes mode, select and move the bones in the spout to make sure they work as hoped, then edit the envelopes further if necessary.

10. Select the nub bone in the spout bone chain, click Animation on the menu bar, point to IK Solvers, click HI Solver, then click the first bone in the spout bone chain.

11. In the Perspective viewport, use Auto Key to animate the teapot spout by animating the goal display in the IK chain, then play the animation. Figure 13 shows an example of what the teapot might look like during the animation.

12. Save the file as **TeaDance**, then reset 3ds Max.

FIGURE 13
Example of completed Project Builder 1

PROJECT BUILDER 2

You are part of a team working on a video game in which the characters move throughout an amusement park. The characters are going to be able to interact with an animatronic fortune teller in the park. Your job is to create the bones for the fortune teller so that its movement can be animated. You plan to work with a low-resolution model as you create and animate the skeletal rig, and then you'll apply the MeshSmooth modifier to the model once animation is complete.

1. Open MAXWB08-01.max from your Data Files drive and directory, select the character in the scene, type **Character** in the Selection Set text box on the Main toolbar, then press [Enter].

2. Right-click the character, click Properties on the Transform quadrant of the Quad menu, deselect the Show Frozen in Gray check box in the Display Properties group, click OK, then freeze the character object.

3. Create a bone chain in the center of the character containing one bone within the torso, two in the neck, one in the head, and a nub bone; then move, rotate, and otherwise adjust the bones so that they conform to the character's physical posture, as shown in Figure 14.

4. Starting from the tip of the torso bone, create a bone chain for the character's left arm containing a bone within the shoulder, one within the upper arm, one within the forearm, one within the hand, and a nub bone. Move, rotate, and otherwise adjust the bones to conform with the curve of the arm, as shown in Figure 15.

FIGURE 14
Bones in torso, neck, and head

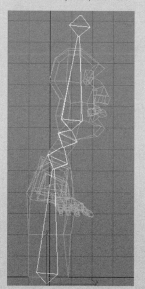

FIGURE 15
Arm bones conform to curve of arm

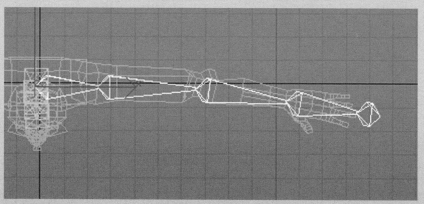

5. Select the arm bone chain (if necessary), click Character on the menu bar, click Bone Tools, click the Mirror button in the Bone Tools group on the Bone Tools floater, then click OK in the Bone Mirror dialog box to create a bone chain in the character's opposite arm that mirrors the one you created. The character's skeletal rig should now look like that shown in Figure 16.

6. Unfreeze the character, then save the file as **FortuneTeller**.

7. Apply the Skin modifier to the character, click the Add button in the Parameters rollout for the modifier, select all of the bones in the Select Bones dialog box, then click Select.

8. Select the head bone, then animate it nodding up and down a couple of times over the active time segment.

FIGURE 16
Completed skeletal rig

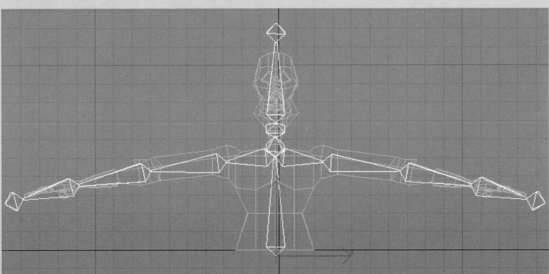

9. Animate each bone in the arm bone chains (except the nub bones) individually so that when the animation is played, the character moves its arms around in different ways.

10. Freeze the character mesh, select all of the bones, type **Bones** in the Selection Set text box on the Main toolbar, then press [Enter].

11. Select the Bones selection set, right-click in the viewport, then click Hide Selection.

12. Unfreeze the character, select it, apply the MeshSmooth modifier to the character, then play the animation. Figure 17 shows what the character might look like as it moves in the animation.

13. Save the file, then reset 3ds Max.

FIGURE 17
Example of completed Project Builder 2

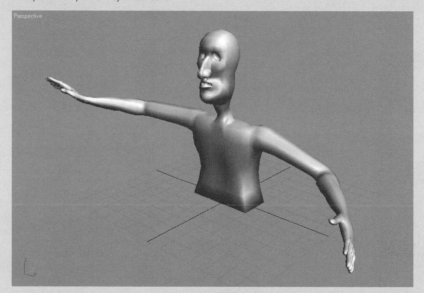

You work for an animation company that is bidding on a project to create an instructional video about sign language. As part of the pitch to the video's producers, you are creating a basic animation of a hand so they can see what it might look like in the video.

1. Open MAXWB08-02.max, select the hand object, type **Hand** in the Selection Set text box, then press [Enter].
2. Open the Object Properties dialog box for the hand object, deselect the Show Frozen in Gray check box, close the dialog box, then freeze the hand object.
3. Turn the grid off in the Perspective viewport, change the viewport to wireframe view, then switch to the Top viewport.
4. Enter bone creation mode; create a bone from below the wrist to the base of the palm; add another to the base of the index finger; add another to the first knuckle of the index finger, another to the tip of the finger; then complete the bone chain with a nub bone beyond the end of the finger.

5. Move the mouse over the wrist bone, click to start another bone chain at the tip of the wrist bone, then create the rest of the bone chain through the end of a second finger.

6. Create three more bone chains leading from the wrist bone through the rest of the fingers on the hand, as shown in Figure 18.

FIGURE 18
Finger bone chains

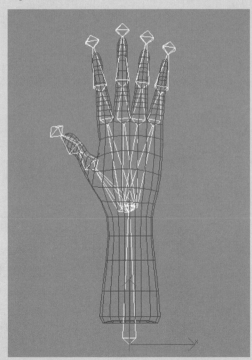

7. Switch to the Perspective viewport, then rotate the bone at the base of the thumb (and others if necessary) so that the bone chain conforms to the shape of the thumb.

8. Enter Bone Edit Mode, adjust the lengths of the bones in the fingers so that the joints (where the tip of a bone meets the base of another) are in line with the knuckles, then move and rotate bones as necessary to make sure the rig conforms to the shape of the hand. (Keep in mind that it is okay for bones to protrude from an object since they do not show up in rendering.)

9. Select the four finger bones connected to the tip of the wrist bone (do not select the thumb bone), then use the Bone Tools Floater to add and size front, back, and side fins to the bones to fill a space similar to the palm they are within.

10. Select the wrist bone, then add and size front, back, and side fins to fill a space similar to that of the wrist they are within. The skeletal rig should now look similar to Figure 19.

FIGURE 19
Completed hand rig

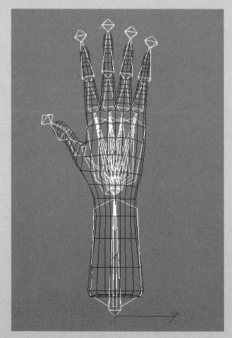

11. Create a selection set containing all of the bones called **Bones**, then save the file as **SignHand**.

12. Unfreeze the hand object, apply the Skin modifier to the hand, add all of the bones to the modifier for the hand, then freeze the hand again.

13. Select the nub bone at the end of the index finger, click Animation on the menu bar,

point to IK Solvers, click HI Solver, then click the bone that leads from the palm to the first knuckle on the index finger.

14. As you did with the index finger, apply the HI Solver to the bone chains within each of the rest of the fingers, including the thumb.

15. Animate the fingers and hand changing into a new position.

16. Select the Bones selection set, right-click in the viewport, click Hide Selection, then play the animation. Figure 20 shows an example of what the animated hand might look like.

17. Save the file, then reset 3ds Max.

FIGURE 20
Example of completed Project Builder 3

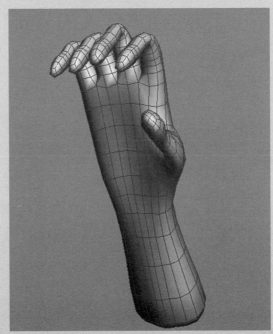

DESIGN PROJECT

You work as a Web designer for a company that is about to roll out a bunch of new Internet services. To call attention to the new services on the company Web site, the marketing manager for the services has asked you to create an animated "i" (as in Internet) that looks like it is dancing and celebrating. Since you know that bones give you great control over how an object changes shape in an animation, you decide to use bones to give life to the "i".

1. Insert a text spline of the letter "i" in the Front viewport, then extrude it to make it three dimensional.

2. Convert the letter into an editable poly, slice it horizontally multiple times to add segments to it and increase its flexibility, then freeze it.

3. Create a bone chain from the bottom to the top of the letter; include at least three bones so that it can bend in a few different places.

4. Apply the HI Solver to the bone chain, with the goal display on the nub bone.

5. Unfreeze the letter, apply the Skin modifier to it, then add all of the bones in the IK chain to the list in the modifier's Parameters rollout.

6. Test how the letter deforms when the bones are moved, then adjust the envelopes of bones as necessary so that the skin deforms the way you want it to.

7. Animate the goal display so that it looks like the letter is dancing to a beat.

8. Create a material for the letter, then apply the material to the letter.

9. Create a plane underneath the letter, create a material for the plane, then apply the material to the plane.

10. Create a target camera in the scene with the letter as its target, convert a viewport to a Camera viewport, then animate the camera's position so that it moves around the letter as it dances.

11. Add a light to the scene that spotlights the letter in the scene.

12. Set the animation to play back in a loop, hide the bones, then play the animation several times.

13. Render the active time segment of the animation to an MOV file called **Letterl** with an output size of 320 × 240.

14. Play the Letterl file in a media player. Figure 21 shows an example of how the letter might look when the file is played.

15. Close the media player, save the scene as **Letterl.max**, then reset 3ds Max.

FIGURE 21

Example of completed Design Project

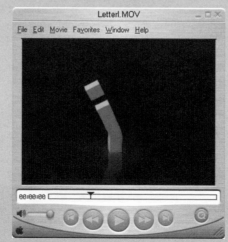
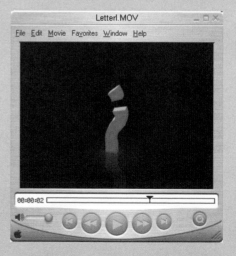

PORTFOLIO PROJECT

You work for an educational software company and are in charge of coming up with a character that will guide students through the activities in a new software product for preschoolers. You decide to use 3ds Max to model the character and create a skeletal rig within the character so that it will be simple to animate.

1. Model a character that would appeal to small children.
2. Create a skeletal rig within the character that enables all of its moving parts to be animated. For instance, in Figure 22, the rig includes bones for the tail, legs, head, and wings.
3. Apply the Skin modifier to the character and add all of the bones in the rig to the modifier's Parameters rollout.
4. Test the effect of bone movement on the character mesh, then edit the envelopes of bones as necessary to eliminate distortion in the character mesh.
5. Animate the bones in the skeletal rig to animate the character's movement.
6. Play the animation in a loop, then save the file as **RiggedCharacter**. An example of a character with a complete skeletal rig is shown in Figure 22.

FIGURE 22
Example of completed Portfolio Project

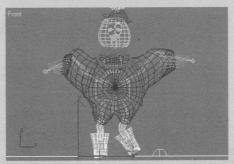

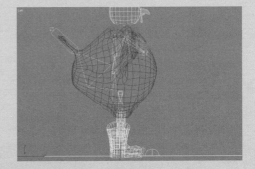

9 PARTICLE
SYSTEMS

1. Work with particle systems.

2. Use space warps.

3. Create materials for particles.

4. Work with Particle Flow.

5. Use material operators.

CHAPTER SUMMARY

In this chapter, you learned what a particle system is and created non-event-driven particle systems such as Spray, Super Spray, and Blizzard. You also adjusted the parameters of particle systems, created and modified space warps, and practiced binding objects in a scene to a space warp. You applied materials to a particle system and modified the particle type to optimize the particles' appearance. You also explored, in depth, 3ds Max's event-driven particle system, Particle Flow; used the components of Particle Flow; and added events in Particle View. You added operators and tests to a particle flow to control the behavior of particles through an animation, and you applied materials that change over time to particles.

FIGURE 1

Rendered particle system bound to space warps

SKILLS REFERENCE

to do this:	use this method:
Add an event to an empty flow or add a new event to a standard flow in Particle View	Drag an operator or test out of the depot and drop it in the events display
Add an operator or test to an event in Particle View	Drag the operator or test from the depot and drop it anywhere in the event **or** Right-click an event, point to Insert or Append on the right-click menu, then click the desired action on a submenu to insert or append it
Adjust the basic parameters of a Snow or Spray particle system	Adjust the parameters in the Parameters rollout on the Modify panel
Adjust the basic parameters of a Super Spray, Blizzard, PArray, or PCloud particle system	Adjust the parameters in the Basic Parameters, Particle Generation, and/or Particle Type rollouts on the Modify panel
Apply a material to a non-event-driven particle system	Drag a material from the Material Editor to a particle in the system or its emitter

to do this:	use this method:
Apply animated materials to particles in an event in Particle View	Add the Material Dynamic operator to the event, select a material, then apply the material to the particles using the operator's parameters panel
Apply material to every face in a particle system containing Facing particles	Select the material in the Material Editor, select the Face Map check box in the Blinn Basic Shader Parameters rollout, then apply the material to the particle system
Apply nonanimated materials to particles in an event in Particle View	Add a Material Static operator to the event, select a material, then apply the material to the particles using the operator's parameters panel
Change the appearance of a material applied to a particle over time	Assign the Particle Age map to a material, adjust the colors and age percentages in the Particle Age Parameters rollout in the Material Editor, then apply the material to a particle system
Change the standard particle shape	Select the particle system, click the Modify tab, then click the option button for the particle shape you want in the Standard Particles group in the Particle Type rollout
Create a non-event-driven particle system	Click ⬤ on the Create panel, click the list arrow at the top of the panel, click Particle Systems, click the button in the Object Type rollout for the desired particle system type, then click and drag in a viewport to create an emitter

to do this:	use this method:
Create a space warp	Click ≋ on the Create panel, click the list arrow at the top of the panel, click the name of the desired space warp category, click the button for the desired space warp in the Object Type rollout, then click and drag in a viewport to create the space warp icon.
Create an event-driven particle system	Click ◉ on the Create panel, click the list arrow at the top of the panel, click Particle Systems, click the PF Source button in the Object Type rollout, then click and drag in a viewport to create the PF Source
Define the parameters for an operator or test in Particle View	Select the operator or test in an event, then adjust its parameters in the parameters panel
Insert a standard flow or empty flow action into the event display in Particle View	Click the desired action in the depot, drag it to the event display, then release the mouse button
Open Particle View	With the PF Source object selected, click the Particle View button in the Setup rollout on the Modify panel
Wire a test to an event in Particle View	Click the test output that protrudes from the left edge of the test, drag it to the input of the new event, then release the mouse button

Work with particle systems.

1. Open MAXWB09-01.max from the drive and directory where your Data Files are stored.
2. Click the Create tab (if necessary), click the Geometry button (if necessary), click the list arrow under the Geometry button, then click Particle Systems.
3. Click the Blizzard button in the Object Type rollout, then click and drag in the Top viewport to create a rectangular emitter that covers the buildings in the city and the three streetlights, as shown in Figure 2.
4. In the Front viewport, move the emitter so that it is above the highest building in the city, then click the Play Animation button to view how the particle system operates with its current parameters.
5. Click the Stop button to stop the animation, move the time slider to frame 0, make sure the emitter is selected, then click the Modify tab.
6. In the Viewport Display group in the Basic Parameters rollout on the Modify panel, click the Mesh option button and change the Percentage of Particles value to **100**.
7. Open the Particle Generation rollout, change the Speed to **5** in the Particle Motion group, change the value in the Use Rate box to 20 in the Particle Quantity group, then change the Emit Start to **–170** and the Emit Stop to **150** in the Particle Timing group.
8. In the Particle Timing group, change the Life value to **170** or a similar number so that the particles reach from the emitter to just below the ground in the city scene in the Front viewport, as shown in Figure 3.
9. In the Particle Size group, change the Grow For value and the Fade For value each to **0**.
10. Open the Particle Type rollout, click the SixPoint option button in the Standard Particles group, then save the scene as **CityBlizzard**.

FIGURE 2
Blizzard emitter in Top viewport

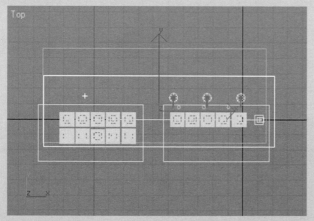

FIGURE 3
Blizzard particles with Life value adjusted

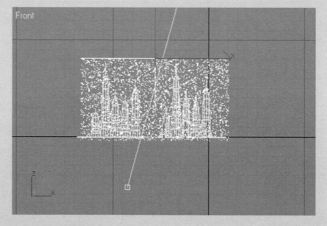

Use space warps.

1. Click the Create tab, click the Space Warps button, make sure Forces appears in the list box at the top of the Space Warps panel, then click the Wind button in the Object Type rollout.

2. Click and drag in the Front viewport to create a space warp emitter to the right of the city scene, click the Select and Rotate tool, then rotate the space warp icon so that its direction arrow is pointing into the city scene, as shown in Figure 4.

3. Click the Bind to Space Warp button; click the particle system; roll the mouse pointer over the particle system until you see the Bind to Space Warp icon; click and drag a line from the Blizzard to the Wind space warp object until you see the Bind to Space Warp icon; then release the mouse button.

4. Select the space warp (if necessary), click the Modify tab, then change the Strength value to **.05** in the Force group in the Parameters rollout.

5. Move the Blizzard emitter to the right in the Front viewport so that the particles fill the area around the street lamps in the city scene, as shown in Figure 5.

6. Click in the Perspective viewport, play the animation to see how the particles look, then stop the animation and save the scene as **CityBlizzard01**.

FIGURE 4
Rotated Wind space warp

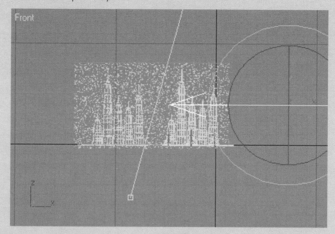

FIGURE 5
Moved Blizzard particle system emitter

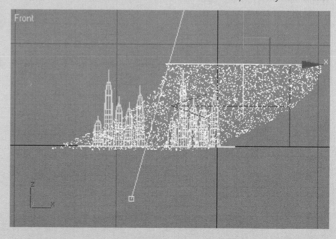

Create materials for particles.

1. Open the Material Editor, select the 07 – Default sample slot, then rename it **Snow**.

2. Click the Diffuse color swatch in the Blinn Basic Parameters rollout, select white in the Color Selector, click the Close button, then click the 2-sided check box in the Shader Basic Parameters rollout.

3. Select the particle system in the scene (if necessary), then click the Assign Material to Selection button in the Material Editor to assign the Snow Material to the Blizzard particles.

4. Click in the Perspective viewport, play the animation to see the effect on the snow, stop the animation, then save the file as **CityBlizzard02**.

5. Click Rendering on the menu bar, click Render, then click the Range option button in the Time Output group. Enter **50** as the start of the range and **75** as the end of the range to render, click the 320 × 240 button in the Output Size group, click the Files button in the Render Output group, then save the rendered output as a .AVI file named **CityBlizzard** in your Data Files drive and directory. Click OK in the AVI File Compression Setup dialog box, then click the Render button in the Render Scene dialog box.

6. Play the AVI file, as shown in Figure 6, then close the media player, close the Render Scene dialog box and rendered scene window in 3ds Max, and reset the workspace.

FIGURE 6
Image from rendered AVI file

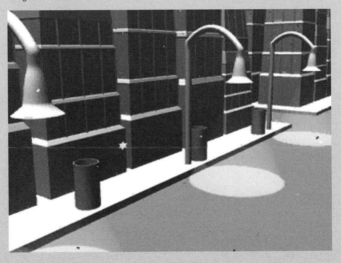

Work with Particle Flow.

1. Open MAXWB09-02.max from the drive and directory where your Data Files are stored.
2. Click the Geometry button on the Create panel (if necessary), click the list arrow below the Geometry button, then click Particle Systems.
3. Click the PF Source button in the Object Type rollout, click and drag to create a small square PF Source emitter in the Top viewport at the location where the water leaves the faucet, move the emitter in the Perspective viewport so that it is located at the end of the faucet, then move the time slider to frame 30. Your scene should look like Figure 7.
4. Click the Modify tab, change the Viewport % value in the Quantity Multiplier group in the Emission rollout to **100**, click the Particle View button in the Setup group, then adjust the size of the Particle View window so that you can see the entire standard flow in the event display.
5. Click the Birth operator in Event 01 in the event display, then in the parameters panel, change the Emit Start value to **30**, the Emit Stop value to **70**, and the Amount value to **100**.
6. Click the Shape operator in Event 01, click the list arrow in the parameters panel, then click Sphere.

7. Click the Display operator in Event 01, click the list arrow in the parameters panel, click Geometry, move the Particle View window (if necessary) so the Perspective viewport is visible, then play the animation.
8. Select the Shape operator again, change the Size value in the parameters panel to **3**, select the Birth operator again, change the Amount value to **50**, then play the animation in the Perspective viewport.
9. Stop the animation, minimize Particle View, create a long and thin cylinder, apply a yellow material to it, then position it horizontally under the particle system emitter so that the particle stream passes through it before reaching the sink.

FIGURE 7
PF Source and particles in Perspective viewport at frame 30

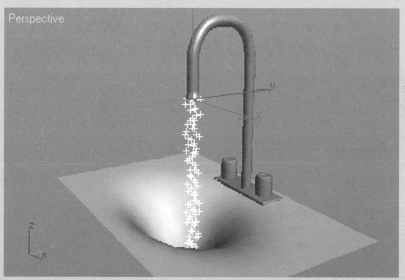

10. Click the Space Warps button on the Create panel, click the Space Warps list arrow, click Deflectors, click the UDeflector button in the Object Type rollout, then click and drag in the Top viewport to create a deflector in the scene.

11. In the Basic Parameters rollout for the deflector, click the Pick Object button, click the cylinder in the scene, click the Bind to Space Warps button on the Main toolbar, click and drag from the deflector to the particle system, then release the mouse button.

12. Restore Particle View, then click and drag the Collision test from the depot to the bottom of Event 01 in the events display.

13. Select the Collision test in Event 01, click the Add button on the parameters panel, then click the deflector in the scene to add it to the Deflectors list.

14. In the Test True if Particle group on the parameters panel, click the Speed list arrow under the Collides option button, then click Continue.

15. Drag the Spawn test from the depot to the events display to create a new event; select the Spawn test in the event; then, on the parameters panel, click the Delete Parent check box, enter **3** as the Offspring #, change the Inherited % in the Speed group to **75**, and change the Scale Factor % in the Size group to **40**.

16. Click and drag from the wire icon next to the Collision test in Event 01 to the Event 02 event input, then release the mouse button to wire the events together.

17. Click the Display operator in Event 02, click the Type list arrow on the parameters panel, then click Geometry.

18. Save the file as **Faucet**, maximize the Perspective viewport, zoom in on the cylinder where the particles collide with it, then move the time slider to frame 70. The viewport and Particle View at this point should resemble Figure 8.

FIGURE 8
Particle system at frame 70 and Particle View

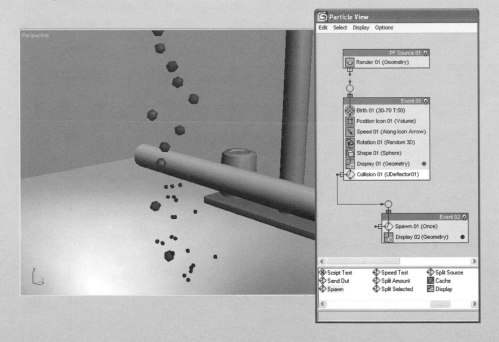

Use material operators.

1. Click and drag the Material Static operator to the bottom of the Birth event in Particle View, then release the mouse button to append the operator to the event.

2. Select the Material Static operator, click the button under the Assign Material check box in the parameters panel, then double-click the Standard material in the Material/Map Browser.

3. Open the Material Editor, click and drag the Assign Material button from the parameters panel to the 07 – Default sample slot in the Material Editor, then click OK to copy the material as an instance to the slot.

4. Select the material sample slot, change the Opacity in the Blinn Basic Parameters roll-out to **6**, change the Specular Level to **75**, then change the Glossiness to **40**.

5. Open the Maps rollout in the Material Editor, click the Refraction map button, double-click the Raytrace map in the Material/Map Browser, then click the Background button to show the colored background in the sample slot.

6. Click and drag the Material Static operator from the Depot to the bottom of Event 02, release the mouse button to append it, select the Material Static operator, click the Assign Material button on the parameters

panel, click the Matl Editor option button in the Browse From group on the left side of the Material/Map Browser, then double-click the material used in the Event 01 Material Static operator to apply it to the spawned particles.

7. Close the Material Editor, save the scene as **Faucet01**, then render a frame in which lots of particles are visible. The scene, and Particle View, should resemble Figure 9.

8. Close Particle View and the rendered scene window, then reset 3ds Max.

FIGURE 9
Particle View and particle system rendered at frame 70

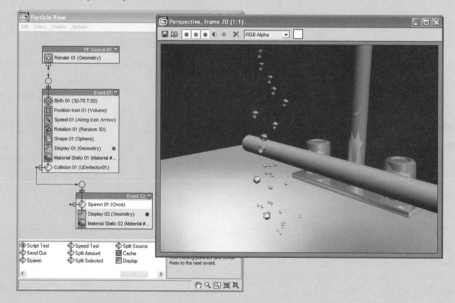

PROJECT BUILDER 1

You are in your first job for an animation company and know that you'll be working a lot with particle systems in your work. You decide to practice creating a basic particle system affected by a space warp.

1. Click the Geometry list arrow, click Particle Systems, click the Super Spray button in the Object Type rollout, then click and drag in the center of the Top viewport to insert a Super Spray emitter.
2. Move the time slider to frame 40, click the Modify tab, change the first Spread value to **10** and the second Spread value to **180** in the Particle Formation group in the Basic Parameters rollout for the system, then click the Mesh option button and change the Percentage of Particles value to **100** in the Viewport Display group.
3. Open the Particle Generation rollout, change the Emit Start to **–100** and the Emit Stop to **150**, then change the Variation of the Life value to **10**.
4. Use the Particle Size group to increase the size of the particles in the system to **3** with a variation of **25**%, then set the Grow For value to **10** and the Fade For value to **0**.
5. Use the Particle Type group to change the particle type to Sphere.

6. Create a Gravity space warp in the Top viewport next to the particle system, bind the space warp to the particle system, then change the Strength of the space warp to **.4**.

7. Create a plane in the Top viewport under the particle system, then rotate and move the particle system so that it looks like Figure 10.

FIGURE 10
Rotated and moved particle system

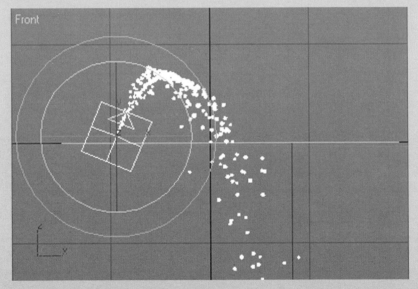

8. Create a UDeflector space warp in the Top viewport, click the Pick Object in the deflector's Basic Parameters rollout, then click the plane.

9. Bind the UDeflector space warp to the particle system, then play the animation in the Perspective viewport. Your Front and Perspective viewports should resemble those shown in Figure 11.

10. Save the scene as **System1**, then reset 3ds Max.

FIGURE 11

Completed Project Builder 1

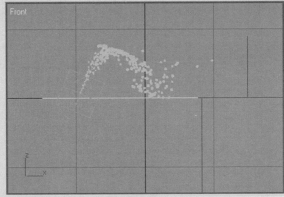

You work for a special effects company that has been asked to create an effect for an animated movie. The effect is the slow appearance of shimmering dust, rising upward in a spiral. In the movie, this dust will rise around a magical character whenever she appears. You plan to create a sample to present to the movie production company of what you think the dust should look like.

1. Create a helix in the Top viewport with a Radius 1 of **40**, a Radius 2 of **20**, a Height of **145**, and a Turns value of **3**.

2. Create a small Blizzard particle system emitter in the Front viewport, then reposition and/or rotate the emitter so that the point from which the particles emanate in the emitter is aligned with the bottom end of the helix.

3. Click the Space Warps button on the Create panel, click the Space Warps list arrow, click Forces, click the Path Follow button in the Object Type rollout, then click and drag in a viewport to insert the space warp into the scene.

4. In the Basic Parameters rollout for the space warp, click the Pick Shape Object button, then click the helix in the scene.

5. Bind the space warp to the Blizzard particle system, then play the animation to view the particle system follow the path of the helix.

6. Select the Blizzard particle system; use the Basic Parameters rollout for the system to display **100**% of the particles in the viewport; use the Particle Generation rollout to change the Speed to **2.2**, the Emit Start to **0**, the Emit Stop to **80**, the Life to **40**, and the Size to **4.5**; then use the Particle Type rollout to change the particle type to Facing.

7. Select the space warp; then, on the Modify panel, change the Travel Time to **60** and the Variation to **50** in the Motion Timing group.

8. Create a material in the Material Editor with a light yellow Diffuse color; click the Face Map check box in the material's Shader Basic Parameters rollout; then assign the Gradient map to its Opacity component. Then, in the Gradient Parameters rollout for the map in the Material Editor, select the Radial option button for the Gradient Type, select the Turbulence option button in the Noise group, and change the Amount in the Noise group to **.5**.

9. Apply the new material to the particle system; play the animation in the Perspective viewport, as shown on the left in Figure 12; then save the file as **Dust**.

10. Render the active time segment as an AVI file called **Dust** with 640 × 480 resolution, then play the AVI file, as shown on the right in Figure 12.

11. Close the media player, then reset 3ds Max.

FIGURE 12
Completed Project Builder 2

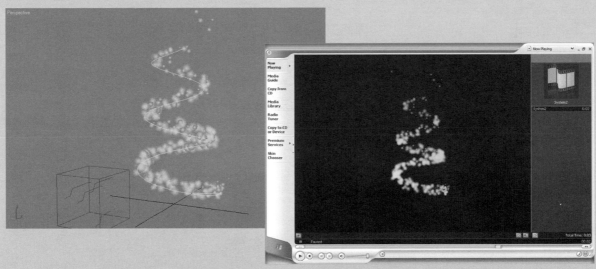

PROJECT BUILDER 3

You work for an advertising agency and are creating the animation for a television commercial for a chain of pet stores. You need to create an animated backdrop for the commercial on which information about the store can be superimposed. The focus of the commercial is on the range of fish and aquarium supplies that are available, so you are creating an underwater scene for the backdrop.

1. Open MAXWB09-03.max from the drive and directory where your Data Files are stored.
2. In the Top viewport, create a PF Source positioned at the bottom of the box, sized similarly to the bottom of the box, then rotate the PF Source so that its direction arrow is aimed at the closed lid of the box.
3. Create a UDeflector in the scene, click the Pick Object button in the deflector's Basic Parameters rollout, click the lid of the box, then bind the UDeflector to the particle system.
4. Select the PF Source, click the Particle View button on the Modify panel, then resize the Particle View window (if necessary) to see all the contents of the event display.
5. Drag the Collision Spawn test from the depot to the bottom of the Birth operator,

release the mouse button, select the Collision Spawn test, click the Add button on the parameters panel, then click the deflector in the scene.
6. Play the animation to view the effect on the particles. As shown in Figure 13, the particles that collide with the lid of the box bounce away.

7. Select the Birth operator, change the Emit Start to −20 and the Emit Stop to 30, select the Shape operator, change the shape of the particles to Sphere and the Size to 10, click the Display operator, change the display type to Circles, select the Collision Spawn test, then change the Offspring # to 2.

FIGURE 13
Particles bounce off deflector after collision

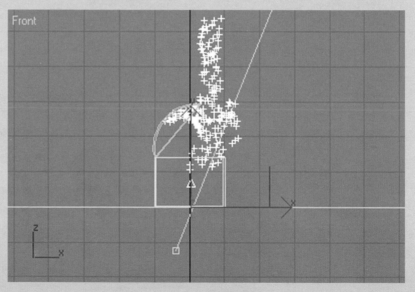

8. Insert a Material Static operator between the Shape and Display operators in the Birth event, select the Material Static operator, then assign the Bubble material from the Material Editor using the parameters panel.

9. Create a Drag space warp and a Gravity space warp in the scene, then bind each to the particle system.

10. In Particle View, drag the Force operator from the depot to an empty spot in the event display to create Event 02, release the mouse button, select the Force operator, then add the Drag space warp and the Gravity space warp to the operator using the parameters panel.

11. Add a Shape operator to Event 02 under the Force operator, select the Shape operator, then change the shape of the spawned particles to Sphere and the Size to **5**.

12. Add a Material Static operator to Event 02 under the Shape operator, select the Material Static operator, then assign the Bubble material to it.

13. Add a Collision test to Event 02, then add the UDeflector to the test on the parameters panel.

14. Wire Event 01 to Event 02, then play the animation in the Perspective viewport.

15. Stop the animation, save the scene as **TreasureChest**, move the time slider to frame 45, then render the scene. Your scene and Particle View should look like Figure 14.

16. Close the rendered scene window, then reset 3ds Max.

FIGURE 14
Completed Project Builder 3

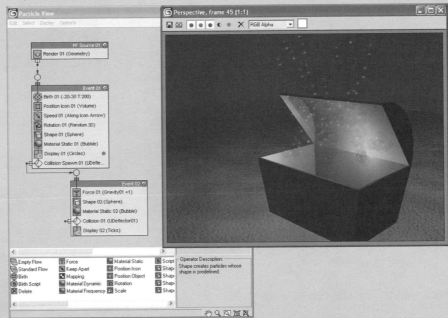

DESIGN PROJECT

A local artist has contacted you for a free-lance job to help her plan out her next project. She is designing a new installation that sprays water into the air in the middle of a plaza that hundreds of people pass through every day. She wants you to help her get a sense of how the water will look in the plaza without people around, and plan the height of the spray of water as well.

1. Model a nozzle for water to come out from, then position the nozzle on a large plane facing upward.

2. Create a Super Spray particle system in the scene, then position it within the nozzle, pointed out of the nozzle.

3. Change the Particle Type for the particles in the system to MetaParticles, then adjust the particle system parameters as necessary to get the look you want for the particles as they move within the system.

4. Create a Gravity space warp in the scene, then bind it to the particle system.

5. Create a material and apply it to the particles in the system to give it the look and refraction qualities of water.

6. Create materials for the nozzle and the plane, then apply them to the nozzle and plane.

7. Add lighting to the scene that lights the fountain and the plane.

8. Create a camera in the scene, convert a viewport to a Camera viewport with Safe Frames active, then aim the camera at the fountain from above and to the side.

9. Animate the movement of the camera slightly, so that it is aimed at the lower part of the fountain at the start of the scene, and at the upper part of the fountain at the end of the scene.

10. Save the scene as **Fountain**, render frames 20 to 30 of the scene as an AVI file called **Fountain**, then open the file and view it in a media player, as shown in Figure 15.

11. Close the media player, then reset 3ds Max.

FIGURE 15
Example of completed Design Project

PORTFOLIO PROJECT

You have been hired for a freelance job to prepare an animation for a drug manufacturer's promotional video on how a drug works. The animation demonstrates how the drug travels through the blood stream and interacts with the body. You decide to use particles to represent the drug and work with Particle Flow to transform the particles onscreen.

1. Open MAXWB09-04.max from the drive and directory containing your Data Files.
2. Create and model a shape to represent the particles of the drug in the bloodstream, then name the object **Particle**.
3. Create a PF Source in the scene and position it so that it appears offscreen to the left in the Perspective viewport and is aimed at an angle down the vein, then set the parameters as desired, such as the number of particles, speed, and so on.
4. Use a Shape Instance operator in the Particle Flow to shape the particles like the Particle object you created.
5. Create deflectors for the boxes on each side of the vein and link them to the particle system.
6. Create a material in the Material Editor that uses a Particle Age map to change the material's color twice over the lifespan of the particle it's applied to.
7. Use a Material Dynamic operator in the Particle Flow that applies the material created in Step 6 to the particles.

8. Use the Collision Spawn test in Particle Flow to have the particles, upon collision with the deflectors, produce one smaller particle that travels through the walls of the vein into the body.
9. Create a new event that changes the shape of the spawned particles to something other than the Particle object, add a Delete operator to the new event that deletes the particles after a Life Span of **10** with a variation of **10**, then wire the Collision Spawn test to the new event.
10. Create a material to apply to the spawned particles, then use a Material Static operator to apply it to the particles.

11. Make final adjustments to the animation timing and particle system parameters as desired, then save the file as **DoseDemo**.
12. Move the time slider to a point in the animation where both the original particles and spawned particles are visible, then render the frame. Figure 16 shows an example of what the scene and the Particle View window might look like.
13. Close the rendered scene window, close Particle View, then reset 3ds Max.

FIGURE 16

Example of completed Portfolio Project

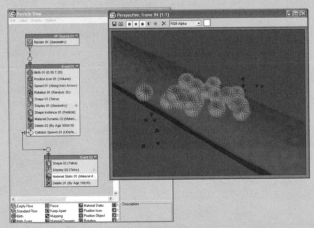

chapter **10** EFFECTS

1. Add atmospheric effects.

2. Adjust atmospheric effect parameters.

3. Understand rendering effects.

4. Apply lens effects.

5. Apply depth-of-field and blur effects.

6. Apply hair and fur.

CHAPTER SUMMARY

In this chapter, you learned about atmospheric effects, added them to scenes, limited some effects to a confined area, applied effects to individual objects, and adjusted effect parameters. You learned what rendering effects are, added them to a scene, and previewed rendering effects in the rendered scene window as you added and adjusted them. You learned about the different types of lens effects, added them to scenes, applied them to lights using the Effects panel, and applied them to other objects by using a common object or material ID number. In addition, you gained an understanding of multi-pass rendering effects and used them to add realism to a scene. You used several methods for blurring objects in a scene. Lastly, you used the Hair and Fur modifier to create hair on an object, adjust its initial parameters, and style and cut the hair once created.

FIGURE 1

Rendered scene containing fire effects, volume light, fog, and lens effects

SKILLS REFERENCE

to do this:	use this method:
Activate Depth-of-Field multi-pass rendering for a camera	Select the camera, click the Enable check box in the Multi-Pass Effect group in the Parameters rollout for the camera, click the Effect list arrow, then click Depth of Field (if necessary)
Activate motion blur multi-pass rendering for a camera	Select the camera, click the Enable check box in the Multi-Pass Effect group in the Parameters rollout for the camera, click the Effect list arrow, then click Motion Blur
Add a rendering effect to a scene	Click the Add button at the top of the Effects rollout on the Effects panel, click the desired rendering effect in the Add Effect dialog box, then click OK
Add an atmosphere to a light object	Select the light object, click the Add button in the Atmospheres & Effects rollout on the Modify panel, click the desired effect in the Add Atmosphere dialog box, then click OK **or** Open the Environment panel, click the Add button in the Atmosphere rollout, click the desired effect in the Add Atmospheric Effect dialog box, click the Pick Light button in the effect's parameters rollout, then click the light object in the scene
Add an atmosphere to an apparatus	Select the apparatus, click the Add button in the Atmospheres & Effects rollout on the Modify panel, click the desired effect in the Add Atmosphere dialog box, then click OK **or** Open the Environment panel, click the Add button in the Atmosphere rollout, click the desired effect in the Add Atmospheric Effect dialog box, click the Pick Gizmo button in the effect's parameters rollout, then click the apparatus in the scene

to do this:	use this method:
Adjust the parameters of a lens effect element	Select the element on the right side of the Lens Effects Parameters rollout, then adjust the parameters in the rollout that appears under the Lens Effects Globals rollout
Adjust the parameters of an atmospheric effect	Select the effect in the Atmospheres rollout list on the Environment panel to open the effect's parameters rollout, then adjust the parameters as desired **or** Select an apparatus or light object, select the effect in the Atmospheres & Effects rollout list on the Modify panel, click the Setup button under the list, then adjust the parameters on the Environment panel
Apply a lens effect element to a scene	Select Lens Effects in the Effects list on the Effects panel, click the name of the element on the left side of the Lens Effects Parameters rollout, then click > to move the effect to the right side of the rollout
Apply a lens effect element to an object	Select the element on the right side of the Lens Effects Parameters rollout, click the Pick Light button in the Lens Effects Globals rollout, then click a light in the scene
Apply hair only on a portion of a model	Select the Hair and Fur modifier in the modifier stack; select the Face, Polygon, or Element subobject level; select the subobjects on the model on which you want hair to appear; then click the Update Selection button in the Selection rollout on the Modify panel

to do this:	use this method:
Apply hair to a model	Select the model, then apply the Hair and Fur modifier to the model
Assign a Material ID number to a material	Click and hold the Material effects channel button in the Material Editor, point to the number that you want to assign, then release the mouse button
Assign an Object ID number to an object	Right-click the object, click Properties on the Transform quadrant of the Quad menu, then assign a number to the Object ID field in the Properties dialog box
Assign an Object ID or Material ID number to a lens effect element	Click the Options tab in the effect's parameters rollout on the Effects panel, select the Object ID or Material ID check box, then change the number in the Object ID or Material ID box
Brush hair	Enter Brush mode, click ▦ (if necessary), then drag the mouse pointer over the hairs to be brushed
Change the name of a rendering effect	Edit the text in the Name field in the Effects rollout on the Effects panel
Create an atmospheric apparatus	Click ◎. on the Create panel; click the list arrow at the top of the panel; click Atmospheric Apparatus; click the BoxGizmo, SphereGizmo, or CylGizmo button in the Object Type rollout; then click and drag in a viewport as you would to create a box, sphere, or cylinder

to do this:	use this method:
Cut hair	Select the hair that you want to cut, enter Brush mode, move the brush over the portion of the hairs to be cut, then press [C]
Display changes to rendering effects as you make them in the rendered scene window	Select the Interactive check box in the Preview group on the Effects panel
Drag hair	Enter Drag mode, click (if necessary), then drag the mouse pointer to drag the hairs
Enable Image motion blur for an object	Right-click the object, click Properties, select the Enabled check box in the Motion Blur group in the Object Properties dialog box, click the Image option button, open the Renderer tab in the Render Scene dialog box, then select the Apply check box (if necessary) in the Image Motion Blur group **or** Add the Blur effect to the Effects list on the Effects panel
Enable Image motion blur or Object motion blur during rendering	Open the Renderer tab in the Render Scene dialog box, then make sure that the Apply check box is selected in the Object Motion Blur group or the Image Motion Blur group
Enable Object motion blur for an object	Right-click the object, click Properties, select the Enabled check box in the Motion Blur group in the Object Properties dialog box, click the Object option button, open the Renderer tab in the Render Scene dialog box, then select the Apply check box (if necessary) in the Object Motion Blur group

to do this:	use this method:
Enter Brush mode in the Style dialog box	
Enter Drag mode in the Style dialog box	
Enter Select mode in the Style dialog box	Press [Esc] to exit the current mode, then click and drag a circular region in the window over the hairs you want to effect
Open the Effects panel in the Environment and Effects dialog box	Click Rendering on the menu bar, then click Effects
Open the Environment panel in the Environment and Effects dialog box	Click Rendering on the menu bar, then click Environment
Open the Style dialog box	Select the Hair and Fur modifier, open the Tools rollout on the Modify panel, then click the Style Hair button
Preview multi-pass rendering effects in the viewport	Click the Preview button in the Multi-Pass Effect group in the Parameters rollout for a selected camera

to do this:	use this method:
Remove a lens effect element from a light	Select the light in the list to the right of the Remove button in the Lens Effects Globals rollout, then click the Remove button
Remove an atmosphere from a light object	Select the light in the list to the right of the Remove Light button in the effect's parameters rollout, then click the Remove Light button
Remove an atmosphere from an apparatus	Select the apparatus in the list to the right of the Remove Gizmo button in the effect's parameters rollout, then click the Remove Gizmo button
Rotate hairs	In Brush or Drag mode, click ![icon], then drag left or right in the Style dialog box
Scale hairs	In Brush or Drag mode, click ![icon], then drag left or right in the Style dialog box
Select all vertices in hair strands	![icon]
Select any hair vertices within the selection region	![icon]
Select hair strands by the vertices at their roots	![icon]

SKILLS REFERENCE

to do this:	use this method:
Select only the end vertices of hair strands	⮌
Show all rendering effects in the Effects list in the rendered scene window	Click the All option button in the Preview group on the Effects panel
Show only rendering effects highlighted in the Effects list in the rendered scene window	Click the Current option button in the Preview group on the Effects panel
Toggle off and on the display of rendering effects in the rendered scene window	Click the Show Original/Show Effects toggle button in the Preview group on the Effects panel
Update the rendered scene window with changes to rendering effects	Click the Update Effect button below the Interactive check box in the Preview group on the Effects panel
Update the rendered scene window with changes to rendering effects and changes to the scene itself	Click the Update Scene button below the Interactive check box in the Preview group on the Effects panel

Add atmospheric effects.

1. Open MAXWB10-01.max from your Data Files drive and directory.

2. Click the Helpers button on the Create panel, click the list arrow under the Helpers button, then click Atmospheric Apparatus.

3. Click the SphereGizmo button in the Object Type rollout, then click and drag from the center of the teapot in the Top viewport to create a spherical atmospheric apparatus about the size of the teapot.

4. Move the apparatus up in the Top viewport so that its center is slightly above the center of the teapot, then move the apparatus up in the Front viewport so that its center is even with the teapot's center.

5. Click the Modify tab, click the Add button in the Atmospheres & Effects rollout, click Fire Effect in the list in the Add Atmosphere dialog box, click OK, then render the Perspective viewport at frame 40, as shown in Figure 2.

6. Close the rendered scene window, then save the file as **Explode**.

FIGURE 2
Fire effect in rendered scene

Adjust atmospheric effect parameters.

1. Select Fire Effect in the list in the Atmospheres & Effects rollout for the apparatus, click the Setup button below the list, pan down the Environment and Effects dialog box to the Fire Effect Parameters rollout, then click the Explosion check box in the Explosion group.

2. Click the Setup Explosion button next to the Explosion check box, change the Start Time to **30** and the End Time to **100** in the Setup Explosion Phase Curve dialog box, click OK, then close the Environment & Effects dialog box.

3. Insert an omni light into the scene, move it above the scene, clone eight instances of the light, then arrange them as shown in Figure 3.

FIGURE 3
Omni lights added to scene

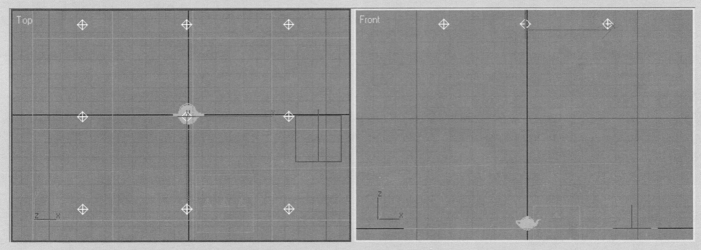

4. Change the multiplier for the lights to **.1**, turn shadows on for the lights, then open the Shadow Parameters rollout for the lights and select the On check box in the Atmosphere Shadows group.

5. Save the file as **Explode01**, move the time slider to frame 40, then render the Perspective viewport, as shown on the left in Figure 4.

6. Move the time slider to frame 75, then render the Perspective viewport, as shown on the right in Figure 4.

FIGURE 4
Explosion fire effect at frames 40 and 75

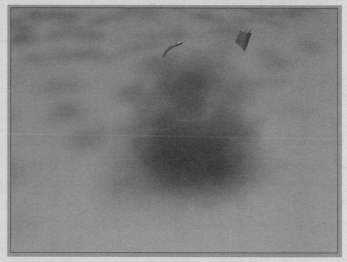

Apply lens effects.

1. Insert an omni light at the center of the atmospheric apparatus in the scene.
2. Click Rendering on the menu bar, click Effects, click the Add button at the top of the Effects rollout, then double-click Lens Effects in the Add Effects dialog box.
3. Click Streak in the list on the left side of the Lens Effects Parameters rollout, click the right arrow button to move it to the right side of the list, pan down to the Lens Effects Globals rollout, click the Pick Light button in the Light group, then click the new omni light in the scene.
4. Click Glow in the list on the left side of the Lens Effects Parameters rollout, click the right arrow button to move it to the right side of the list, pan down to the Lens Effects Globals rollout, click the Pick Light button in the Light group, then click the new omni light in the scene.
5. Close the Environment and Effects dialog box, then save the file as **Explode02**.
6. Move the time slider to frame 20, then render the frame. Note that when an object is in front of a light with a lens effect applied to it (as the teapot is in front of the omni light when whole), the lens effect does not appear.
7. Move the time slider to frame 35, then render the Perspective viewport as shown on the left in Figure 5.
8. Move the time slider to frame 65, then render the Perspective viewport as shown on the right in Figure 5.
9. Close the rendered scene window.

FIGURE 5
Lens effects rendered at frames 35 and 65

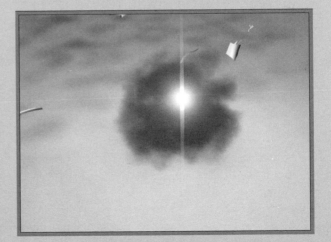

Apply depth-of-field and blur effects.

1. Click in the Perspective viewport, click Views on the menu bar, click Create Camera from View to insert a target camera in the scene, then adjust the camera's target in the Top and Front viewports so that it is closer to the center of the atmospheric apparatus.

2. Maximize the Camera viewport, move the time slider to frame 40, select the camera (if necessary), click the Modify tab, then click the Enable check box in the Multi-Pass Effect group to enable the Depth-of-Field rendering multi-pass effect.

3. Change the Sample Radius to **5** in the Depth-of-Field Parameters rollout, then return to the Multi-Pass Effect group and click the Preview button to preview the depth-of-field effect in the Camera viewport. The viewport should look similar to Figure 6.

4. Select the camera again (if necessary), click the list arrow in the Multi-Pass Effect group, then click Motion Blur.

5. In the Sampling group in the Motion Blur Parameters rollout, change the Duration (frames) value to **5**, then click the Preview button in the Multi-Pass Effect group. The viewport should look like Figure 7.

6. Save the file as **Explode03**, then reset 3ds Max.

FIGURE 6
Depth-of-Field multi-pass effect previewed in viewport

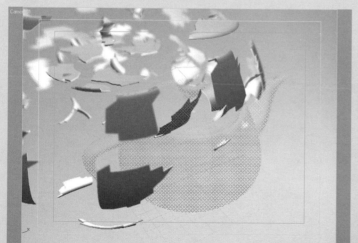

FIGURE 7
Motion Blur multi-pass effect previewed in viewport

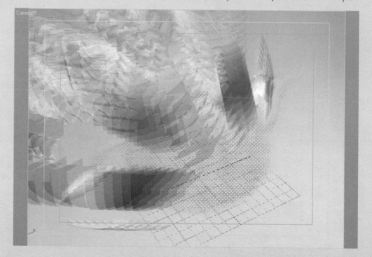

Apply hair and fur.

1. Open MAXWB10-02.max from your Data Files drive and directory, then select the character object.
2. Click the Modify tab, click the Modifier List list arrow, then click Hair and Fur to apply it to the character.
3. Click the Polygon button in the modifier's Selection rollout, click in the Left viewport, select the polygons on the character's head as shown in Figure 8, then click the Update Selection button in the Selection rollout.

4. Click the Style Hair button in the Tools rollout for the modifier, then click and drag down over the character's hair to brush it downward so that the hairs are stretched to full length.
5. Press [B] and drag down in the viewport to reduce the brush to about a half inch in diameter, click the Select any hair strand by its root button, drag the roots of the hair in front of the character's face so that there are no guide hairs in front of its eyes,

then brush other hairs as necessary to make all of the hair hang straight down.
6. Click the Done button, rotate the Perspective view so that the front of the character is in its center, then save the file as **CharacterHair**.
7. Render the scene. Your scene should resemble Figure 9.
8. Close the rendered scene window, then reset 3ds Max.

FIGURE 8
Selected polygons for hair

FIGURE 9
Rendered hair

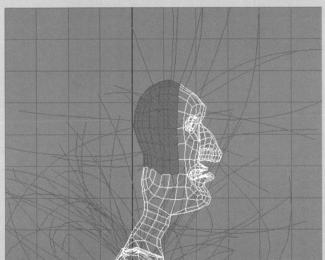

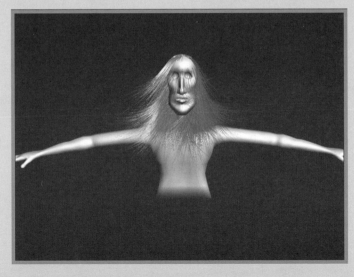

You have presented to a production company a sample effect for an animated movie the company is making. The effect is a spiral of shimmering dust rising upward around a magical character whenever she appears. The company likes the sample and has asked you to add some glow to the dust in the sample as well as an area of fog that surrounds the dust and the appearing character. To do this, you plan to add a lens effect and an atmospheric effect to the scene.

1. Open MAXWB10-03.max from your Data Files drive and directory.

2. Open the Material Editor, select the upper left sample slot if necessary, click the Material ID Channel button, then click 3.

3. Close the Material Editor, open the Effects panel in the Environment and Effects dialog box, click the Add button in the Effects rollout, then double-click Lens Effects in the Add Effect dialog box.

4. In the Lens Effects Parameters rollout, move the Glow lens effect element from the left to the right side, then select the Glow element on the right side.

5. Pan down to the Glow Element rollout, change the Size to **.05**, change the Intensity

to **50**, click the Options tab, select the Material ID check box, change the Material ID number to **3**, then close the Environment and Effects dialog box.

6. Click the Helpers button, click the list arrow under the Helpers button, click Atmospheric Apparatus, then create a large spherical atmospheric apparatus around the helix, as shown in Figure 10.

7. Open the Environment panel in the Environment and Effects dialog box, click the Add button in the Atmosphere rollout, then double-click Volume Fog.

FIGURE 10
Atmospheric apparatus added to scene

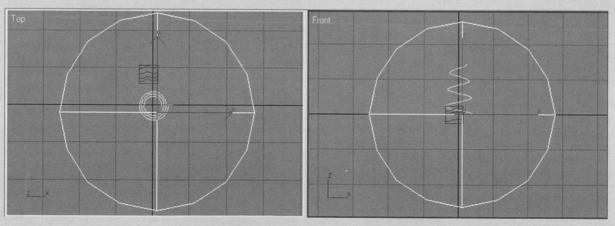

8. Select Volume Fog in the Atmosphere list, pan down to the Volume Fog Parameters rollout, click the Pick Gizmo button in the Gizmos group, then click the apparatus in the scene.

9. Change the Density to **1.5**, click the Turbulence option button and the Bottom option button in the Noise group, then close the Environment and Effects dialog box.

10. Save the file as **FogDust**, move the time slider to frame 50, then render the Perspective viewport. Your scene should look similar to Figure 11.

11. Close the rendered scene window, then reset 3ds Max.

FIGURE 11
Rendered scene with glowing particles and volume fog

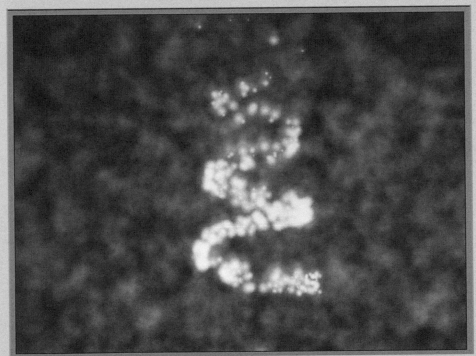

PROJECT BUILDER 2

You work at a cinematic effects company and are bidding for the work on an independent drama. There are some basic animations that need to be done for the intro sequence at the start of the film. You need to demonstrate to the filmmakers how you can easily create dramatic lighting effects and a unique cinematic style, so you are creating a sample file that uses effects to accomplish this.

1. Create a box in the top viewport, apply the Normal modifier to the box to reverse the normals, then create a teapot resting on the bottom of the box.
2. Create and apply light-colored materials for the box and teapot, then apply them to the objects.
3. Add a spotlight to the scene aimed at the teapot from above.
4. Add a target camera to the scene aimed at the spout of the teapot, then position the camera so that it is close to the spout of the teapot.
5. Convert a viewport into a Camera viewport, then adjust the camera position further, if necessary, so that the teapot is in closeup in the Camera viewport.

6. Open the Environment panel of the Environment and Effects dialog box, then add the Volume Light effect to the list in the Atmosphere rollout.
7. Pan down in the dialog box to the Volume Light Parameters rollout, click the Pick Light button, then click the spotlight in the scene.

8. Change the Density to **3**, click the Noise On check box, change the Amount to **.5**, then close the Environment and Effects dialog box.
9. Render the Camera viewport. The scene should look similar to Figure 12.

FIGURE 12
Rendered scene with Volume Light

10. Close the rendered scene window, select the camera, then position the camera's target close to the top of the teapot on the spout side.

11. Enable the Depth-of-Field multi-pass effect for the camera in the Parameters rollout, with a Total Passes amount of **15** and a Sample Radius of **2**.

12. Preview the multi-pass rendering effect in the Camera viewport, as shown in Figure 13.

13. Save the file as **Closeup**, then reset 3ds Max.

FIGURE 13

Preview of Depth-of-Field effect in Camera viewport

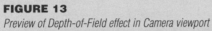

PROJECT BUILDER 3

As a freelance animator, you have been hired to create an animation for a funky hair salon showing a head with an unusual hairstyle from the point of view of a camera moving slowly around the head. The animation will be edited together with other animations and played in their front window. You've created the head, and now you need to add the hair to the head, light the scene, and animate it.

1. Open MAXWB10-04.max from your Data Files drive and directory.
2. Add a target camera to the scene aimed at the center of the head object from a position below the nose on the right side of the head; animate the position of the camera so that it moves slowly from the right side of the head toward its front; then create a Camera viewport for the camera.
3. Select the head object, then apply the Hair and Fur modifier to it.
4. On the Modify panel for the modifier, click the Face button, activate the Left viewport, use the Lasso Selection Region tool on the Main toolbar to select faces on the head in a shape resembling a natural hairline, then update the selection.
5. Open the Tools rollout, click the Load button in the Presets group to open a window showing several preset hair types, then double-click the clumpy-wet-brown.shp file in the upper left of the window to use as the hair for the head.
6. Open the Effects panel of the Environment and Effects dialog box, select the Hair and Fur modifier in the Effects rollout list, click the list arrow in the Hair and Fur rollout further down in the dialog box, then click Geometry.
7. Minimize the Environment and Effects dialog box, then render the Camera viewport.
8. Add three spotlights to the scene above and behind the head that are aimed at the bottom of the scene (and don't light the head). The cones of at least a couple of the spotlights should be visible in the camera viewport throughout the animation.

9. Add the same Volume Light effect to each of the spotlights.
10. In the Volume Light Parameters rollout, color the fog in the volume light a very light green color, change the Density to **3**, change the Max Light % to **100**, then change the Sample Volume % to **8** (deselect the Auto check box first).
11. Save the file as **SalonHair**, then render the Camera viewport at frame 100. An example of the rendered scene is shown in Figure 14.

FIGURE 14

Example of completed Project Builder 3

DESIGN PROJECT

You work in the design department of a publishing company and have been asked to create the cover for a new children's chapter book in which characters go through multiple adventures as they seek a magic lantern. Because the lantern is not actually shown in the book, you get to design the look for the lantern to use on the cover, and use effects to give it an extraordinary appearance.

1. Create and apply material to a plane on which the lantern will sit.

2. Model a container (lantern) for the candle to rest within, create and apply materials to the container so that it has clear glass walls within the lantern's frame, then insert a light above the lantern to light the lantern and its surrounding area.

3. Model and apply appropriate materials to a small candle resting at the bottom of the lantern, then insert a light at the end of the candle's wick.

4. Add a Volume Light effect to the candle's light, then adjust the effect's parameters to create a smoke-like appearance for the light, including using the parameters in the Noise group of the Volume Light Parameters rollout.

5. Add two lens effect elements to the candle's light and adjust their parameters to create the look of intense brightness.

6. Insert a target camera in the scene, then use Depth-of-Field multi-pass rendering to focus on the area from which the candle's light shines. Preview the effect in the Perspective viewport. An example of what the previewed scene might look like is shown in Figure 15.

FIGURE 15
Example of Depth-of-Field effect previewed in viewport

7. Save the file as **Candle**, disable the multi-pass rendering effect for the camera in the scene, then render the scene at 320×240 resolution. An example of a completed Design Project is shown in Figure 16.

8. Close the rendered scene window, save the scene, then reset 3ds Max.

FIGURE 16
Example of completed Design Project

PORTFOLIO PROJECT

As a level designer for a new video game based in a metropolis, you have created a city environment in which the characters of the new game will interact. You need to add details to the scene to make the city look populated and busy on a snowy night. You plan to use lens effects to light windows in the buildings, and several other effects to add realism to the scene.

1. Open MAXWB10-05.max from your Data Files drive and directory.

2. Create a light yellow material in the Material Editor, then assign a Material ID number to it.

3. Assign the material to several randomly located polygons in the buildings in the city scene.

4. Add the Glow lens effect element to the material using its Material ID number, then adjust the element's parameters to get the effect of windows glowing at night.

5. Add the Volume Light effect to the spotlights in the streetlamps, then adjust the parameters of the effect as desired.

6. Create a blizzard particle system that adds falling snow to the scene, apply a white material to the particles, then use a blurring effect to blur the snowflakes as they fall.

7. Use the Depth-of-Field multi-pass effect to focus the view on the base of the middle streetlamp, then preview the effect in the viewport.

8. Add layered fog to the lower part of the scene to give it a misty look.

9. Save the file as **CityNight**, then render the Camera viewport. An example of what your scene might look like is shown in Figure 17.

10. Close the rendered scene window, then reset 3ds Max.

FIGURE 17

Example of completed Portfolio Project

CAPSTONE PROJECT (CHAPTERS 1-10)

You work for an animation company that has a major department store as a client. You are developing a virtual information booth the store is considering having installed in locations throughout its stores. An interactive character will be located in the virtual information booth and will help customers find what they are looking for in the store. You are designing the character and the décor around the information booth, animating the character, lighting the scene, and rendering two frames from the animation to give to the store as examples of what is possible for the information booth.

1. Open MAXWBCAP-01.max from your Data Files directory. This file contains the virtual information booth to be used in the animation.
2. Model a character (torso, head, arms, and hands) that will be located in the center of the information booth. Create eyes in the character's head that can rotate independently. Make the character look as realistic as possible. Use materials to create the look you want.
3. Add bones to the character to create a rig for it that conforms to its shape.
4. Include hair and clothing on the character. Use materials to create the look you want.

5. Add lighting to the scene focused on the character, and add lighting that lights the booth and background. Use effects to enhance the look of the scene.
6. Add two cameras to the scene: one that views the character in close-up, and another that is aimed at the information booth from further out. Use a Camera viewport for each.
7. Animate the character doing something that a person at an information booth would do when interacting with a customer.

CAPSTONE PROJECT (CHAPTERS 1-10)

8. Add particle systems to the columns behind the information booth to add movement to the décor.

9. Render two single frames as TIF files (named **Char1.tif** and **Char2.tif**) from the start of the animation and the end of the animation, each from a different camera. An example of a completed Capstone Project is shown in Figure 1. Save the scene as **CharCapstone**, then reset 3ds Max.

FIGURE 1

Example of completed Capstone Project

Read the following information carefully!

This section contains two lists:

- **Autodesk 3ds Max 8 Revealed Projects Workbook Data Files** lists the Data Files necessary to work through the projects in this book.

- **Autodesk 3ds Max 8 Revealed Data Files** lists the Data Files necessary to work through the lessons in the main textbook.

Find out from your instructor the location where you will store your files. To complete many of the chapters in this book, you need to use the Data Files provided under this ISBN at *www.course.com*. Your instructor will tell you what drive and directory on your computer or server you will be copying the Data Files to. Your instructor will also tell you where you will store the files you create and modify.

Copy and organize your Data Files.

- Use the Data Files List to organize your files to a zip drive, network folder, hard drive, or other storage device.

- Create a subfolder for each chapter in the location where you are storing your files, and name it according to the chapter title (e.g., Chapter 1).

- For each chapter you are assigned, copy the files listed in the **Data File Supplied** column into that chapter's folder.

Find and keep track of your Data Files and completed files.

- Use the **Data File Supplied** column to make sure you have the files you need before starting the chapter indicated in the **Chapter** column.

- Use the **Student Creates File** column to find out the filename you use when saving your new file for the exercise.

DATA FILES LIST

Data Files List
Autodesk 3ds Max 8 Revealed Projects Workbook

Chapter	Data File Supplied	Student Creates File	Used In
1		Practice01	Skills Review
		Practice02	Skills Review
		Practice03	Skills Review
	MAXWB01-01.max		Skills Review
2		Standard Primitives	Skills Review
		Standard Primitives01	Skills Review
		Standard Primitives02	Skills Review
		Standard Primitives03	Skills Review
		Standard Primitives04	Skills Review
		Standard Primitives05	Skills Review
		Standard Primitives06	Skills Review
		Standard Primitives07	Skills Review
		Ziti	Project Builder 1
		Teatime	Project Builder 2
		Glazed	Project Builder 3
		Street	Design Project
		Solar System	Portfolio Project
3		Cane	Skills Review
		Normals	Skills Review
		Building	Skills Review
		Terrain	Skills Review
		Egg	Skills Review
		BoxTwist	Skills Review
		Handwrist	Skills Review
		Closedspline	Skills Review
		Goblet	Skills Review
		Decanter	Project Builder 1
		Chessking	Project Builder 2
		Rabbitman	Project Builder 3
		Glassware	Design Project
		Flashlight	Portfolio Project

Chapter	Data File Supplied	Student Creates File	Used In
4		MaterialSamples	Skills Review
		MaterialSamples01	Skills Review
		MaterialSamples02	Skills Review
		MaterialSamples03	Skills Review
		MaterialSamples04	Skills Review
		FallingLeaf	Project Builder 1
	Leaf_diffuse.jpg		Project Builder 1
	Leaf_opacity.jpg		Project Builder 1
	Address.tif	AddressPlate	Project Builder 2
		GlassExamples	Project Builder 3
		UFOSighting	Design Project
		Asteroids	Portfolio Project
5	MAXWB05-01.max	BoxTable01	Skills Review
		BoxTable02	Skills Review
		BoxTable03	Skills Review
		BoxTable04	Skills Review
	MAXWB05-02.max	LampRoom	Project Builder 1
	MAXWB05-03.max	FlashlightOn	Project Builder 2
	MAXWB05-04.max	CityNightCam1	Project Builder 3
		CityDayCam2	Project Builder 3
		Chandelier	Design Project
		Strategy	Portfolio Project
6	MAXWB06-01.max	Eyes01	Skills Review
		Eyes02	Skills Review
		Eyes03	Skills Review
		Eyes04	Skills Review
		Eyes05	Skills Review
		Eyes06	Skills Review
		Eyes07	Skills Review
		Eyes08	Skills Review
	MAXWB06-02.max	FighterJet	Project Builder 1
	Top.tif		Project Builder 1

Chapter	Data File Supplied	Student Creates File	Used In
		Camera Tunnel	Project Builder 2
		BouncingBall	Project Builder 3
		Dart	Design Project
		Maze	Portfolio Project
7	MAXWB07-01.max	RenderedGlass	Skills Review
		Glass.avi	Skills Review
		Glass0010.jpg – Glass0015.jpg (6 files)	Skills Review
		RenderedGlass01	Skills Review
		Glass.tif	Skills Review
		RenderedGlass02	Skills Review
	MAXWB07-02.max	Chandelier.tif	Project Builder 1
		Chandelier.jpg	Project Builder 1
	MAXWB07-03.max	DartboardTV.avi	Project Builder 2
		DartboardWeb.mov	Project Builder 2
	MAXWB07-04.max	360 Degrees	Project Builder 3
		/RoomSequence/CameraView0001.jpg – CameraView0100.tif (100 files)	Project Builder 3
	MAXWB07-05.max	StrategyCard.tif	Design Project
		StrategyWeb.jpg	Design Project
	MAXWB07-06.max	JetBackground.avi	Portfolio Project
	Top.tif	JetBackground.max	Portfolio Project
		JetFly.avi	Portfolio Project
		JetFly.max	Portfolio Project
8		CylinderBones	Skills Review
		CylinderBones01	Skills Review
		CylinderBones02	Skills Review
		CylinderBones03	Skills Review
		CylinderBones04	Skills Review
		CylinderBones05	Skills Review
		TeaDance	Project Builder 1
	MAXWB08-01.max	FortuneTeller	Project Builder 2

Chapter	Data File Supplied	Student Creates File	Used In
	MAXWB08-02.max	SignHand	Project Builder 3
		LetterI.max	Design Project
		LetterI.mov	Design Project
		RiggedCharacter	Portfolio Project
9	MAXWB09-01.max	CityBlizzard	Skills Review
		CityBlizzard01	Skills Review
		CityBlizzard02	Skills Review
		CityBlizzard.avi	Skills Review
	MAXWB09-02.max	Faucet	Skills Review
		Faucet01	Skills Review
		System1	Project Builder 1
		Dust	Project Builder 2
		Dust.avi	Project Builder 2
	MAXWB09-03.max	TreasureChest	Project Builder 3
		Fountain	Design Project
		Fountain.avi	Design Project
	MAXWB09-04.max	DoseDemo	Portfolio Project
10	MAXWB10-01.max	Explode	Skills Review
		Explode01	Skills Review
		Explode02	Skills Review
		Explode03	Skills Review
	MAXWB10-02.max	CharacterHair	Skills Review
	MAXWB10-03.max	FogDust	Project Builder 1
		Closeup	Project Builder 2
	MAXWB10-04.max	SalonHair	Project Builder 3
	EYE_DIF.psd		Project Builder 3
	FACE_MAP.psd		Project Builder 3
		Candle	Design Project
	MAXWB10-05.max	CityNight	Portfolio Project
Capstone Project	MAXWBCAP-01.max	CharCapstone	
		CapCamera1_scene.avi	
		CapCamera2_scene.avi	

Data Files List

Autodesk 3ds Max 8 Revealed

Chapter	Data File Supplied	Student Creates File	Used In
1		Myfile01	Lesson 1
		Myfile02	Lesson 1
	MAX01-01.max	MAX01-01	Lesson 2
	MAX01-02.max		Lessons 5-7
2		Selection Tools	Lesson 2
		Two Spheres	Lesson 2
		Rotate Object	Lesson 3
		Scale Object	Lesson 3
		Box Param	Lesson 4
		Sphere Param	Lesson 4
		Cone Slice	Lesson 4
		Segments	Lesson 5
		Modifiers	Lesson 6
		Clones	Lesson 7
		Tapered Spheres	Lesson 7
		Array	Lesson 7
		Link Pyramids	Lesson 8
		Cylinder Pivot	Lesson 9
		Rotate Links	Lesson 9
		Snapping Cone	Lesson 10
		Align Objects	Lesson 11
3		Editpoly	Lesson 1
		Modifypoly	Lesson 2
		Viewnormal	Lesson 3
		Extrudepoly	Lesson 4
		Extrudevert	Lesson 4
		Bevelpoly	Lesson 4
		Paintdef	Lesson 5
		Softselect	Lesson 5
		Createconnect	Lesson 6
		Weldvert	Lesson 6

Chapter	Data File Supplied	Student Creates File	Used In
		Bridgepoly	Lesson 6
		Meshsmooth	Lesson 7
		Modelref	Lesson 7
		Symteapot	Lesson 7
		XRefscene	Lesson 7
	MAX03-01.max	Character	Lesson 8
		Extrudespline	Lesson 11
		Lathespline	Lesson 11
		Loftdeform	Lesson 11
4		Materials	Lessons 1-2
		ShinyMaterial	Lesson 3
		AssignMap	Lesson 4
		NavigateMap	Lesson 5
		Mapparam	Lesson 6
		Bumpymap	Lesson 7
		Filter	Lesson 7
5		Camerascene01	Lesson 1
		Camerascene02	Lesson 1
		Camerascene03	Lesson 2
		Camerascene04	Lesson 2
		Camerascene05	Lesson 2
		Lightscene01	Lesson 3
		Lightscene02	Lesson 3
		Lightscene03	Lesson 3
		Lightadjust01	Lesson 4
		Lightadjust02	Lesson 4
		Lightadjust03	Lesson 4
		Lightadjust04	Lesson 4
		Lightadjust05	Lesson 4
		Lightadjust06	Lesson 4
		Shadowscene01	Lesson 5
		Shadowscene02	Lesson 5

Chapter	Data File Supplied	Student Creates File	Used In
		Advancedlight01	Lesson 6
		Advancedlight02	Lesson 6
6	MAX06-01.max	Toy Plane	Lesson 1
	MAX06-02.max	Toy Plane02	Lesson 2
	MAX06-03.max	Toy Plane03	Lesson 3
	MAX06-04.max	Toy Plane04	Lesson 4
	MAX06-05.max	Toy Plane05	Lesson 5
		Sphere Animation	Lesson 6
		Curve Edits	Lesson 6
	MAX06-07.max*	Toy Plane07	Lesson 7
	MAX06-08.max	Toy Plane08	Lesson 8
7	MAX07-01.max	Table	Lesson 2
	MAX07-02.max	Starfighter.max	Lesson 4
		Starfighter.avi	Lesson 4
		/sequence/Starfighter0000.jpg – starfighter 0150.jpg (151 files)	Lesson 4
		[variable].max	Lesson 5
		[variable].tif	Lesson 5
8		Createbone	Lesson 1
	MAX08-01.max	Dragonbird	Lessons 1-6
9		Particle1	Lesson 1
	MAX09-01.max	Waterfall	Lessons 2-3
	MAX09-02.max	Missiles	Lessons 4-5
10	MAX10-01.max	Torchscene	Lessons 1-4
	MAX10-02.max	Pylons	Lesson 5
	MAX10-03.max	Bullet	Lesson 5
		Bullet.avi	Lesson 5
	MAX10-04.max	Hair	Lesson 6
Appendix	Example_RandObjects.ms		Lesson 2
		BentBox.ms	Lesson 2
		Terrain.ms	Lesson 2
	Macro_FileBrowser.ms		

*No MAX06-06.max Data File or Toy Plane 06 Solution File due to mistake in numbering.

NOTES

NOTES

NOTES

NOTES